JOSEPH HARRIS

THE 40 DAY

GOD RUNNERS

HIS WORD IS HIS CREED

FORTY DAYS AS A GOD RUNNER
TO TRANSFORM AND WIN 40 SOULS INTO GOD'S KINGDOM

By

JOSEPH HARRIS

JOSEPH HARRIS

Copyright © 2017 The 40 Day God Runners By Joseph Harris

All rights reserved

Artwork by Can Stock

Editing and Cover Design by

Destiny House Publishing, LLC

www.destinyhousepublishing.com

inquiry@destinyhousepublishing.com

P.O. Box 19774

Detroit, MI 48219

ISBN#1936867281

ISBN 13 # 978-1936867288

JOSEPH HARRIS

DEDICATION

This book is inspired and dedicated to my Father in Heaven, my father and mother, Joe Arthur Doyle and Gussie Doyle.

Thank God for my parents introducing me to Jesus Christ. My prayer is that my parents rejoice in Heaven before God's throne. My father and mother were responsible for my baptism in the name of the Father, Son and the Holy Ghost (Matthew 28). I thank God that both of them had the right mind to get their children in relationship with our Lord, Jesus Christ.

I believe both of them knew the power of God. I credit them for guiding me in the right direction of life. This helped me to get on the right path and began my journey, walk and service as a kingdom servant of Jesus Christ. Thanks to God who helped me walk away from the dark side of life. I could have been dead and gone if it had not been for the Lord on my side. If it had not been the Lord in the life of my parents, who knows which direction I would have taken. God led my parents to guide me to Jesus.

JOSEPH HARRIS

CONTENTS

DAY		PAGE
	Prayer	8
	Purpose	9
1	The God Runner	11
2	Mind of Christ	15
3	A Second Chance God	18
4	Claim Your Gift Through Prayer	22
5	Identity Factor	26
6	Deliverance, Let My People Go!	29
7	Blood Washed	32
8	God Looks at the Heart of Man	35
9	God Called You to Bless You	39
10	His Will Be Done	42
11	Save Your Family From the Flames	45
12	He is Coming Again	48
13	Love Your Brother	51
14	God is My Foundation	54
15	Holy Spirit Filled	57
16	The Mind of Christ	60

17	Find Grace In God's Eyes	63
18	The Spirit Fills Us With Power	66
19	Thou He Slay Me, I Trust Him	69
20	Jesus is the Word	74
21	He is Risen	77
22	Dreams of Blessings	80
23	The Power of Transformation	84
24	Man Under God's Influence	87
25	Bind it and Loose it!	90
26	When God Opens Your Eyes	93
27	Planted by the Rivers of Water	97
28	Power In the Tongue	100
29	Seed Experience	103
30	The Last Trumpet	107
31	Preach Jesus with Power	110
32	He Opens Doors to Bless You	113
33	Fix Your Eyes on God	117
34	God Knows Your Works	122
35	Newness of God	126
36	Abide In Jesus	130

37	If You Knew The Gift of God	134
38	When I See the Blood	137
39	Jesus Helps Me Stand	139
40	Victory is in Jesus Christ	141
	The 40 Day God Runner Fiction Story	145
	About the Author	158

JOSEPH HARRIS

PRAYER

I am a God Runner. I pray to continue to be a God Runner. I also pray that God will change you into a God Runner within the next 40 days, if not sooner. Taste and see that the Lord is good; blessed is the one who takes refuge in him (Psalm 34:8).

I pray that these words will draw me near to God and help add to my life, the goodness of your grace and love (James 4:8).

Father, may all the spiritual scales be removed from my life today so that I can know you better and see those visions that you have predestined for my life.

Today, I surrender to your will and your way. I surrender all to you. I acknowledge and repent of all my sin before you (Acts 3:19). Father, you are the only true and wise God. There is no one like you. You are the only one who can set men free from the bondage of sin that so easily entangles us. Lord, give me understanding in your truth as I encounter these readings.

Help me to rightly divide this word and meditate day and night on your goodness. Your word is alive and active. Sharper than a two-edged sword and can penetrate even to the soul and spirit, joints and marrow; it judges the thoughts and attitudes of the heart (Hebrew 4:12). I pray that your word will not return void (Isaiah 55:11). Father, help me not to be ashamed of the gospel. It is through the power of the word of God that salvation and deliverance are given to those that ask. Lord, I need you to make me over (Romans 1:16).

Create in me a clean heart and renew a right Spirit in me. I am under your construction willing to work to advance the Kingdom of God (Psalm 51).

GOD RUNNERS - 40 DAY BLITZ

PLEASE READ PURPOSE

PURPOSE: This book is intended to encourage those who are called by God to become genuine God Runners that will do amazing things in the sight of God. This book will transform your way of thinking and set a fire inside your soul. You get to be one of God's soul winners for His kingdom. You are blessed by God! You are a true disciple of Jesus Christ. You are doers of the word by faith, not just talkers; deceiving yourself (James 1:22). The God Runner is a prayer warrior and crisis responder for the glory of God. It is my prayer that after 40 days or during the process, every person that reads this book will become a God Runner in Jesus Christ. Every God Runner will win souls and set a goal to win 300 people to Jesus Christ. You can do it for the love of God!

These readings are for every person who needs to know the power of God in their lives. God can transform, heal, restore and work in your life for His glory. He comforts you and strengthens you in all situations. You and I need Jesus in our lives. If you do not have him, read the Bible for it is the primary source over all books. You receive salvation by faith (Romans 10:9), confess and repentance (1 John 1:9) and become born again. God's Word is the motivating factor for this book. God's Word is the key! All words are inspired by the Holy Spirit! You will notice scripture from the Bible in this book for God's glory only.

This book will equip and encourage each witness to be a fisher of men (Mark 4:18-22). This God Runner book is for both men and women to evangelize and witness to other people that are lost.
God's word will help you understand more of His plan (Ephesians 2:1-4; 2:20-21; 3:10-12). These scriptures will also help others to seek Jesus Christ as Lord and Savior (Matthew 6:33), be fruitful (Galatians 5:22-24), live in Christ (Galatians 2:20-21), and become

a God Runner, denying yourself, picking up your cross and following Jesus Christ (Matthew 16:24), while giving all glory and honor to Jesus Christ.

DAY 1

THE GOD RUNNER!

1 Corinthians 9:24 Do you not know that in a race all the runners run, but only one gets the prize? Run in such a way as to get the prize.

All runners that race for God are God Runners! When they run for God they run in a manner pleasing to Him to get the prize. They are highly blessed and favored under His influence. God Runners win multiple souls into the Kingdom. When God Runners move they are motivated to get positive results.

The Olympic Games is a major international multi-sport event. All athletes reveal the peak of their talent in running, swimming, balancing beams, skiing, wrestling, and many other events in an effort to win a gold medal. The athletes have practiced and worked hard for years to get to the point of optimal fitness. The gold medal is on the forefront of each competitor's mind. Second place is not good enough. Anything other than a gold medal may spell defeat in the mind of the participants.

Saints of the Most High God, we are winners in Jesus Christ. God Runners always win people to Jesus Christ. God Runners are led by the Holy Spirit to win every race. I know without a doubt, my plan in Jesus Christ as a witness and disciple, is to win the gold medal He desires for me to win. My friend, it is a crown that He will give His chosen servants much like in Revelation 4. Nevertheless, the crown He gives his servants should be cast to the living Savior. He is the Lamb of God who has redeemed us with His blood. What I achieve in life is to the glory of Jesus Christ. I now take on the attitude of the Apostle Paul. As the He expressed in scripture, I press toward the prize of the high calling of Jesus Christ that I might please Him. I witness because of the glory and blessing of Him who brought me out of darkness into His marvelous light. Saints, the Lord wants all of us to run the race. It is a race to win souls. All of those in God's Kingdom have a mission and obligation to tell of the salvation that Jesus offers. We must tell them that God forgives all of our sins; because Jesus has taken all of it away on the cross. He died for us and rose from the grave with all power. Jesus was raised from the dead by the power of His Father in heaven. He blessed me and empowered me to live right. Therefore, I am a God Runner!

CHOOSE TO LIVE, NOT DIE!

Genesis 1:15 -17 The Lord God placed the man in the Garden of Eden to tend and watch over it. But the Lord God warned him, "You may freely eat the fruit of every tree in the garden except the tree of the knowledge of good and evil. If you eat its fruit, you are sure to die."

The enemy specializes in manipulation. In this story, he shows up and tries to pull God's children away from Him. This explains exactly why God wants God Runners to exist and multiply around the world. God wants men to reconnect with other godly men and their families, but primarily with Himself. He wants to start a Holy Ghost fire inside of them. God will use what He created to get His glory. He will use God Runners. Jesus was a God Runner. We are to follow His example. Jesus was the second Adam who came to give life (1 Corinthians 15:45). God Runners help restore and bless people of God. They pull people from the torment of the devil (Luke 16:23).

God created man all by Himself! The same God gave Adam dominion. Adam did not lack anything. He had the obedience that God wanted inside of man. Adam was entrusted with everything

God had made. He also intended that Adam would take care of the garden and all things that were under his authority and power. God gave Adam a paradise. God has made it where nothing could pluck Adam out of His hands. Nevertheless, He also gave Adam the freedom to choose. Exercising one's own free will is a powerful thing. You can make a choice today to accept Jesus as Lord into your heart and walk in obedience. When you accept Him as Lord, He is your Savior as well. Jesus died on the cross and rose from the dead.

In the beginning, the primary harmful sin that destroyed Adam's position and blessings was the act of disobedience. He ate of the fruit from the tree of knowledge of good and evil, at the hand of his wife. Adam and Eve's disobedience to God symbolizes their broken relationship. They both made a choice to worship the evil one as soon as they rebelled against God. Today, people are still being influenced by the devil. However God reclaimed His people through the sacrifice of Jesus.

When you worship someone in the spirit, usually you bow down before them. God did not create you to bow before the devil. You were created to bow before God only. Adam and Eve obeyed the serpent (the devil) rather than obeying God. The majority of society does the same thing, today, because they are blinded by that devil. Not only did Adam obey Satan, Adam obeyed his wife instead of God by eating of the fruit of the tree of knowledge of good and evil. As a result, sin entered the world. Sin runs rampant because of this first family's act of disobedience.

What is your family like? Adam was given authority to be Eve's covering against all enemies, principalities and wickedness. Eve was not to be the head nor put herself in that position. Adam was positioned as the head by God. The husband is positioned by God as leader of the family. He is supposed to cover the wife and shield her from all enemy attacks; every wife must position herself properly so she can honor God and her husband. She should not make room for any devils! She must be submissive to her own husband! Allow Him to lead the household and not break the order of God. Otherwise the house is out of order. It is important that every man know that Adam was created with the ability to choose obedience in God rather than disobedience. One choice can either make you or break you. He fell, along with his wife, because of rebellion and disobedience. Anytime a person ignores God and does what he pleases, he steps outside of God's covering and authority. He therefore may have altered the blessing God had intended for him. You have the power of free choice, but you need to make the right choice. You should choose Jesus as Lord and Savior.

DAY 2

THE MIND OF CHRIST

1 CORINTHIANS 2:14-17 But the natural man does not receive the things of the Spirit of God, for they are foolishness to him; nor can he know *them,* **because they are spiritually discerned. But he who is spiritual judges all things, yet he himself is** *rightly* **judged by no one. For** *"who has known the mind of the LORD that he may instruct Him?"* **But we have the mind of Christ.**

A new believer will have the mind of Christ. Christians, or real believers, have the mind of Christ. This means that they are converted and born again. This is the only way to get it. We must receive Jesus in our heart as Lord and Savior.

The goal of the born again person is to help the natural man who is lost and heading to hell. The natural man is a man who has not received salvation in Christ Jesus. The natural man has no relationship whatsoever with Jesus Christ. There is no depth of the word of God in him. This natural man is lost in darkness and in his own sinful ways. He fights against the word of God. He has severe hang-ups in his life that keeps him from honoring God. This same thing applies to women that do not have a relationship with God. A natural man is not spirit-filled. He may have the spirit of the enemy and lives by his own flesh. He depends on his fleshly desires, lust and opinions of others. He trusts in false wisdom and those that tell fortunes and deal in witchcraft and false gods. He is stuck on himself and has no intention in getting to know anything about God. He lives and thrives for the lies of Satan and is spiritually blind to evil. However, some do know it but the blindness blocks the reality of deliverance.

When wisdom of God is presented before the natural man, he

does not believe because everything that is of wisdom is foolish in his sight. He cannot comprehend the mind of Christ or the blessings from within the mind of Christ because he is extremely engaged in the secular world. Let's help him before God shows him how much of a fool he really is. He is not stronger than God. It would be foolish of this man to believe that he created the world and all that is inside of it. God did it with His mighty power.

I am reminded of a young man who plays football. Every day he goes to practice and he believes in the playbook that the coach uses to run plays in practice. He never sees the book, but believes in the diagram painted by the coach. He runs the plays effectively in practice. However, he gets hit even harder in practice. God wants us to believe and pass on what we believe in Jesus to others. If an athlete can put all of his belief in a playbook that has no power to save him, why not believe in Jesus' play book that will save us in His everlasting Kingdom? We can, put on the mind of Christ by using the Bible, which is God's playbook. Watch God move in your life.

FORMED, SANCTIFIED & ORDAINED BY GOD!

JEREMIAH 1:5: "Before I formed thee in the belly I knew thee; and before thou came forth out of the womb I sanctified thee, and I ordained thee a prophet unto the nations."

Every man needs to know who is responsible for forming him (Genesis 2:1-7). A Hebrew word is " yatsar (yaw-tsar) which means "through the squeezing into shape; to mold into a form as a potter; It also means to fashion, form, frame, make, and purpose (Dobson et al., 1994)."

In the book of Jeremiah, God emphatically speaks to Jeremiah, informing him that He already knew him before he was formed. It is God making it clear to His prophet, Jeremiah, something that is so profound to the human psyche. God was reassuring Jeremiah that He was on his side, no matter what.

No matter what the battle looks like, God has already predestined it for your success. God set you apart for His purpose and blessed you! No matter how many people come up against you and try to strike fear into your heart God already made you victorious where ever you place the sole of your feet as people of God.

Ask God to form good thoughts and good things in your heart and mind that you would not sin against Him. It is time for you to give yourself to God. Ask God to sanctify you, allow his power to constantly work on the inside of your heart. Ask God to ordain you and set you apart for His purpose on the missionary field and/or in an office of Bishop or as a Prophet or one of the five-fold ministries.

If you want to be serious about getting Jesus in your life, repeat this prayer: Lord, I ask you to give me a new mind, a new spirit, and make me more like you to love others. Help me with identifying who I am in Jesus Christ. Lord, I ask you to come into my heart and be my Savior. I ask for forgiveness of my sin. I believe that you are the Son of God and you died and rose again from the dead. You formed me and blessed me. You set me apart to be used in your Kingdom to glorify your name. Lord, thank you for sanctification; you are working inside my heart. Only God can make prophets like Abraham, Elijah, Elisha, Isaiah, Jeremiah and others.

DAY 3

A SECOND CHANCE GOD!

Acts 9 Saul! Saul! Why are you persecuting me?

Have you ever been persecuted? Persecute means a set or means of punishing or hurting someone. In most cases, those that are persecuting are self-righteous. They believe and are totally convinced that the persecution they commit is right in their eyes. Remember this same great Apostle was once like that. So he knows firsthand the power of a second chance in life with God. This time with God in your life and you on God's side, no enemies in hell, nor on the earth can stop the power of God's blessing on you.

Jesus makes this statement to Saul in his old nature, "Why are you persecuting me?" Really, he had no answer. His response was simply, "Is that you Lord?" This simply tells us that deep down inside his heart, while he was killing people, that he already knew that God was real.

The problem with so many people is that the enemy blinds them in a way to keep them in darkness. The enemy will have you doing things that you never thought you would do. Ask God to remove the blinders and take you out of darkness. Jesus shows us the opposite in His power when He allowed Saul to become temporarily blinded. I believe he did it so that when Saul converted to Paul it would be crystal clear that Jesus was behind his deliverance and conversion. He also moved in his life so that he could ask for mercy and forgiveness in his heart. He also wanted the Apostle to witness personally the power of conversion by sending him to Ananias to lay hands on him and pray so that the scales could fall off of his eyes. Then he could see clearly Jesus in his life.

I believe Jesus is asking us the same question today, "Why are you persecuting me?' In other words, He is saying, "I have been blessing you all of your life. Why do you hate others? Why are you not serving me? Where is the love in your life for others? When will you allow yourself to die to sin and be born again? You must have a conversion." In John 3:3 the scripture says, you must be born again. God will always reveal the second chance and why you need it. God gives second chances in healing. Many people will answer that they have a drug issue, gang violence issue, prostitution issue, pimp issue, a double life issue, failure mentality (God lifts you and encourages you), faith issue (wrong practice in the spirit) and one reason you are having all of these problems and looking for a second chance is that you are not lined up with God. As a God Runner, you need to accept Jesus as Lord and Savior (Romans 10:9).

TRANSFORMED TO DO THE WILL OF GOD

ROMANS 12:1-2: I beseech you therefore, brethren, by the mercies of God, that ye present your bodies a living sacrifice, holy, acceptable unto God, which is your reasonable service. And be not conformed to this world: but be ye transformed by the renewing of your mind, that ye may prove what is that good, and acceptable, and perfect, will of God.

2 CORINTHIANS 11:15 Therefore it is no great thing if his ministers also be transformed as the ministers of righteousness; whose end shall be according to their works.

The Apostle Paul expresses a sense of urgency by stating, "I beseech you, by the mercies of God. Here is a preacher of the gospel basically begging people to hurry up and accept Jesus as Lord and Savior. He is expressing the importance of presenting oneself, which is to be a living sacrifice, holy acceptable unto God. He is saying at least give yourself to God. Make the best choice ever in your life.

He reminds us that we should not seek to emulate those of this world. We should seek to be transformed by the renewing of our minds. Break away from the world's system and old way of life. The Apostle Paul was a sanctified, Holy Ghost filled man! He was a Kingdom man because God called him and did a makeover in his life! God transformed his entire life. The word used in Greek is "metamorpho" which is the root word of metamorphosis, change after being with (meta) (Dobson et al., 1994)." Metamorphosis means change, transfigure and transform (Dobson et al., 1994)."

The Incredible Hulk is a powerful example of what happens in transformation. The butterfly transforms from being a worm to flying and soring with wings is another powerful picture that God shows us. You will be transformed if you let Jesus inside of your heart.

We must be careful of those things in the world that can also transform people. If you desire to be transformed, first of all be like Jesus and His disciples. There are also people that are heroes that transformed this nation like Martin Luther King Jr., Mother Teresa, Rosa Parks, Jesse Owens, Babe Ruth, Hank Aaron, Jackie Robinson, and Jim Brown. There were others: John Calvin and Martin Luther in the Christian world of the reformation. Their theology made an impact and so many other people of various origins and races that made contributions to the world. I don't have room to put all of them in this book.

Most people do not recognize the tricks of the evil one. We need Jesus in order to resist being drawn any deeper into Satan's kingdom. This writing is to rescue you from the grips of the devil and his demons. Repeat this right now! "Lord Jesus, I surrender to you at this very moment. I repent to you and ask that you come into my heart at this moment. I believe you died for my sins and rose on the third day by the power of God. I accept you as Lord in my heart. Thank you. In Jesus name Amen."

Men need to be transformed by the renewing of their minds to get through all attacks. Men need to walk in the spirit of Jesus Christ. Be anointed from head to feet! Every man needs a prayer life. It is every man's duty to protect his wife and children from the attacks of the enemy. He must use the word of God daily for strength, power and his weapon of authority!

Man must present himself to God as a living sacrifice. God does not need a dead sacrifice from you. Jesus paid the price. He was the sacrifice for all mankind. God wants you to live in the spirit and be witnesses on the earth.

You will have the authority to pray and break curses and seductive spirits when you see them approaching your wife. Yes, you guessed it. Men have seductive spirits, as well.

DAY 4

CLAIM YOUR GIFT THROUGH PRAYER

1 CORINTHIANS 12:4-11: There are different kinds of gifts, but the same Spirit. There are different kinds of service, but the same Lord. There are different kinds of working, but the same God works all of them in all men. Now to each one the manifestation of the Spirit is given for the common good. To one there is given through the Spirit the message of wisdom, to another the message of knowledge by means of the same Spirit, to another faith by the same Spirit, to another gifts of healing by that one Spirit, to another miraculous powers, to another prophecy, to another distinguishing between spirits, to another speaking in different kinds of tongues, and to still another the interpretation of tongues. All these are the work of one and the same Spirit, and he gives them to each one, just as he determines. The body is a unit, though it is made up of many parts; and though all its parts are many, they form one body. So it is with Christ. For we were all baptized by one Spirit into one body whether Jews or Greeks, slave or free and we were all given the one Spirit to drink.

Start praying about your gift. The God Runner has gifts and he uses those gifts. The female God Runner also utilizes her gifts. They both are God fearing heroes. This God Runner saves lives. He and she are like Marvel characters such as Captain America, Incredible Hulk, Thor and the others. In the Christian environment and all around the world, the God Runner rescues people from evil and helps them also to receive salvation. In this passage gifts are explained and God wants each God Runner to grab hold of that gift and witness in the Kingdom.

Do you have a relationship with God or with something else? Is it an obsession with sports or a girlfriend up the street? I was once obsessed with football until I woke up one day with an injury. Later I had a spiritual awakening. God had opened my eyes to the fact that a sport has no salvation in it. It does have a high payoff for talent and gifts, but nothing else.

NFL players dig deep within to show their talents of running, catching, passing, blocking and tackling. There is nothing wrong with that kind of raw talent. Some are the best of the best running backs in college and NFL football. If there is anyone who enjoys watching a winning football team that would be me. The point is that talents and gifts are to be used and expressed to their fullest potential.

The Apostle Paul teaches us in Corinthians 12. There are nine gifts in this passage that God made available to every Christian. The point of this passage is to remind us that we are empowered by God to make a difference. The Apostle Paul did not delay in using the gifts that God gave him. He was filled with the Holy Spirit and on fire to use his gifts after being converted.

It is evident that one of his gifts was the message of wisdom and another gift was the message of knowledge. His preaching was superior and bold with fire (Holy Spirit) behind it. The evidence is the Gospel. We know this to be true because the Apostle Paul wrote two-thirds of the gospel with knowledge and wisdom from above. The Apostle explains that God simply gives these gifts as He determines. Then He makes them available for those who will choose to serve Him. If you are not ready and mature enough, He may withhold it until you are ready to be a true servant. The Christian does not decide which gift they want. God decides on your gift. We may desire and ask, but ultimately, He decides. You just receive the gift. Make no mistake there are more gifts than these listed. Please be fully reminded that you are now a God Runner. You have a genuine heart to run for Jesus. Please see 1 Corinthians chapters 12-14; Romans 12; Ephesians 4 and 1 Peter 4. You are under God's craftsmanship and authority to use these gifts. Search God for more in your life. Allow God to get the maximum use of your gifts. Keep in mind that God wants us to know that Jesus is our gift, first and foremost in this life and the life to come. (1 Corinthians 12:1-11).

A GODLY MAN

GENESIS 45. Joseph could not refrain himself before all them that stood by him; and he cried, Cause every man to go out from me. And there stood no man with him, while Joseph made himself known unto his brethren. And he wept aloud: and the Egyptians and the house of Pharaoh heard. And Joseph said unto his brethren, I am Joseph; doth my father yet live? And his brethren could not answer him; for they were troubled at his presence.

It will never matter as to who is around you when God puts joy in your heart because of your love for family. In Joseph's encounter we learn much more than what we see. Joseph automatically demonstrates the power of forgiveness. We know this because of his cry with overwhelming joy to see his brothers (family). The opposite would have been natural, since they had tried to kill him. He had all the power and authority to avenge himself. He was not reflecting on revenge. He was reflecting on the love of God in his life and for his family. There is an unbreakable bloodline connection between brothers even when it looks like the devil has the advantage. The enemy caused them to put Joseph in a pit, and then left him for dead. When God raises you up from the pit, you need to understand that blessings are flowing in your life that you can't even begin to understand. There is a level of favor that God is about to pour out in your life when He pulls you out of that pit.

Joseph was secure enough within himself to reveal to his brothers his identity. It is perfectly fine for a man to show that kind of joy. Joseph wept in his joy! Joseph wept and did not care who would hear him. It was almost like giving God glory and praise for that moment in his life. Joseph could have looked back as a man and realized that God kept him in the midst of trouble, in the midst of jealousy, and in the midst of division. His genuine question as a man could have been, "Doth my father live?" Joseph was a godly man who displayed the highest level of respect for his father, Jacob; as well as the God who blessed his family. There are multiple messages in this scripture that God is showing us. He wants us to know that we can be God Runners that bless our families. God wants us to know that we can recover from any tragedy, mistreatment, hurt, put down, or knock down from the enemy Today, be a God centered man or woman. Meditate on Jesus and ask Him to be your Savior. Read Romans 10:9-10. Enter in the joys of life as a newborn creature in Jesus Christ. You will never be the same again. Look at Joseph. He was never the same again. He had to walk in blessings. You see what the enemy meant for bad, God meant for good. If you want to get close to anybody in this life and trust them completely, get close to Jesus Christ, the Son of the living God.

DAY 5

IDENTITY FACTOR

Matthew 16:13 which states "Whom do men say that I the Son of man am?" The response is located in Matthew 16: 14 which says, "And they said, Some say that thou art the John the Baptist: some, Elias; and others Jeremias, or one of the prophets" Jesus asking another question, Matthew 16:15 "He saith unto them, But whom say ye that I am?" In Matthew 16:16, it says, " And Simon Peter answered and said, thou art the Christ, the Son of the living God. In Matthew 16:17 scripture says, And Jesus answered and said unto him. Blessed art thou, Simon Barjona: for flesh and blood had not revealed this unto you, but my Father which is in heaven (Matthew 16:13-17)." Jesus said in Matthew 16:18 And I say unto thee, That thou art Peter, and upon this rock I will build my church; and the gates of hell shall not prevail against it (Matthew 16:13-18)."

Jesus reminds us that He is responsible for building the church. In this passage, Jesus points out, just as Peter proclaimed Jesus's identity, Jesus comes right back and reveals Peter's identity. In verse 18, Jesus said, and I say also unto thee, thou are Peter and upon this rock, I will build my church, and the gates of hell shall not prevail against it. Jesus is the head of the church. The body of Christ must start recognizing that Jesus is God's appointed agent over the Church. When the body of Christ comes together, the joy of the Lord will come forth. The saints of God will give Him glory. It's because people will finally learn of their true identity, which is in Jesus Christ.

In Matthew Chapter 4, Jesus was in the wilderness and the devil tried to tempt Him by saying if you are the Son of God turn these stones into bread. In verse 4, the response to the devil was "It is written, man shall not live by bread alone, but by every word that proceedeth out of the mouth of God" The enemy's goal was to make Jesus sin and lose his identity. He wanted Jesus to bow down to him. He offered Jesus things in the following verses Matthew 4:1-11. When you know who you are in Jesus Christ, you will walk victorious everywhere you go.

PRAISE BREAKS THROUGH PRISONS!

ACTS 16:25-26: But at midnight Paul and Silas were praying and singing hymns to God, and the prisoners were listening to them. Suddenly there was a great earthquake, so that the foundations of the prison were shaken, and immediately all the doors were opened and everyone's chains were loosed.

God never intended for men to be behind prison bars nor in any form of permanent lock up. People do have seasons in life when they venture off into the wrong directions. Bad choices cause them to get locked up or go to prison. Make sure you understand that we live in a world where all kinds of prisons exist. The most deadly one is a spiritual prison. We were made to live in paradise, not in a prison.

Usually people find themselves in prison due to rebellion and a disobedient spirit. People allow the sin nature to dominate and corrupt their lives. Nevertheless, there are some people that are all about witnessing for the glory of God, but the enemy tries to lock them in prisons unjustly. God in His infinite power and majesty always prevails in the life of the believer.

Paul and Silas were persecuted because they were men of God who spread God's Word. God wants men to be free of whatever mindset and prison you are experiencing in life. Whatever has you on lock down, break it! Break the old past that surfaces to make you feel unworthy! Break the old rules that keep you tied down! Break the traditional man-made rules! Break that Pharisee mentality! The Pharisees did not want to follow Jesus. They were high-minded, prideful and jealous-spirited people. Rebuke that spirit in the name of Jesus! God wants you to be strengthened in His might! Prayer and praise can break all prisons, bondages, and barriers! Men who praise God can really make a difference in breaking prison walls. There is no reason to remain locked in prison in your own mind. You don't have to allow drugs; gang violence and other temptations get a hold of you and damage your life any further. You are a child of the Most High God. You can withstand arrows of the enemy because of the Armor of God. Put every piece on and stand your ground. You can recover from any bad prison experience with God on your side. You are a winner. Jesus Christ is inside your heart. Joseph knew who he was in the Lord this is why the warden in the prison recognized him. **GENESIS 39:23 The keeper of the prison looked not to anything that was under his hand; because the Lord was with him, and that which he did, the Lord made it to prosper**.

My friend when the Lord is with you, no demon in hell can bring you down. Just remain humble and committed in heart. Continue to praise Him and pray. You might experience an earthquake in your life. You have the victory in Jesus Christ.

DAY 6

DELIVERANCE, LET MY PEOPLE GO!

EXODUS 5:1-5: Afterward Moses and Aaron went in and told Pharaoh, "Thus says the LORD God of Israel: 'Let My people go, that they may hold a feast to me in the wilderness.' And Pharaoh said, "Who is the LORD, that I should obey His voice to let Israel go? I do not know the LORD, nor will I let Israel go." So they said, "The God of the Hebrews has met with us. Please, let us go three days' journey into the desert and sacrifice to the LORD our God, lest He fall upon us with pestilence or with the sword." Then the king of Egypt said to them, "Moses and Aaron, why do you take the people from their work? Get back to your labor.

God simply stated to Pharaoh, "Let my people go! People are in bondage right now in America and all around the world. If Pharaoh had only known that the God of Moses and Aaron was the only true and wise God, he may have altered his life sooner. As long as a person has the spirit of Pharaoh, he will be blinded by his own power and pride. He will be self –motivated and will not see God for who He truly is. Pharaoh basically answered no to God, "I will not let Israel go!" The person that takes this attitude will suffer a great deal of loss because he chooses to go against God. When the sovereign Lord God speaks, we must be obedient and hearken to His call. Whenever God sends a messenger, it is incumbent upon us to listen to what thus said the Lord.

Pharaoh met his fate at the Red Sea. It is not like Pharaoh did not have enough chances to surrender to God. Even today, people have that same Pharaoh spirit and will not surrender until God takes something that is precious. You had better wake up now and take to these words! For example, God took Pharaoh's Son and that broke his heart, but at that same time, his heart hardened much more against God.

Deliverance comes from God. Moses's name means deliverance and God used him mightily. He opposes a pharaoh-type mentality. He doesn't want his people living in an emotional or spiritual Egypt. God never intended and is not responsible for His people living that way. That is exactly why He sent Moses to deliver His people from bondage. God specializes in deliverance. Once you read the entire account of what happened in Egypt, then you will understand the absolute power and love of God for His people. God does not allow slavery to destroy Christians. God always gets the attention needed to release His people. He makes a way out of no way. Just as He caused His people to walk through the Red Sea, He will make a way for you. He specializes in turning the impossible into the possible. God delivers whoever calls on the name of Jesus Christ.

A PRAYER FOR DISCIPLES!

John 17:6-7 I have manifested your name to the men whom you have given me out of the world. They were yours. You gave them to me, and they have kept your word. Now they have known that all things which you have given me and from you.

This is powerful because Jesus is praying to the Father in Heaven for the men that God gave Him. This is what we should do in our homes as men, pray over our families. Jesus is showing us an example of what we should do for other people. Jesus is looking for us to be disciples. We are to pray for other Christians that the devil takes his hands off. Instead pray also that God does put his hands on you with multiple blessings. God hears all of Jesus's prayers. Jesus is the advocate for the disciple and today

Jesus is an advocate for prayer at all times. The Holy Spirit is our helper in so many ways. In this scripture, Jesus prayed for his disciples. In verse 20, he prayed for all who will believe in Him. He was speaking directly to His Father in Heaven.

Jesus wanted His disciples to be blessed by the Father. He knows all about who we are and what we desire. If you are a follower of Christ, you can count on the Holy Spirit's prayers on your behalf. The Lord prays for us because He cares. The Lord prayed for God to keep His disciples strong in difficult times. Lord, make me a prayer warrior. Make me a man of God under construction and put the anointing of prayer on my lips that I will become an intercessor!

DAY 7

BLOOD WASHED

Hebrews 9:22 In fact, the law requires that nearly everything be cleansed with blood, and without the shedding of blood there is no forgiveness.

Blessed be the name of Jesus Christ. He is the God Runner for the Father in Heaven. It was Jesus who washed us in His blood. Roman 5:1-5 tells us that we are justified by His blood. The only One that could remove the sting of death is our Lord. The Hebrew writer makes it clear that without the shedding of the blood, there is no remission of sin. We need to understand that this blood has washed us clean! The blood of Jesus has all power. You need to start pleading the blood. Speak the blood because it reminds the enemy of his defeat on Calvary! Declare it! "I am blood washed by the Lamb of God!" Teach your family members to speak the same thing. Why is God revealing this to us? He reveals it because you need to know who you are in Christ and what He did for you. He reminds us over and over that the blood redeemed us from sin.

In 1 Kings 18 Elijah has a show down. God sends fire from heaven to prove He is God on behalf of Elijah's prayer request. Buddha can't forgive you. Hare Krishna can't forgive you, Muhammad can't forgive you, Baal can't forgive you. Not one of them has power to either send fire from heaven or wash your sins away. Jesus blood is the only blood that has power to heal, forgive, restore, and to remove the stain of sin. When Jesus died on the cross, it was finished. He washed all of my sins away. I am cleansed because of Jesus. I can walk in Holiness because of Jesus. He was crucified in His body for my sin! He died and was buried then was raised from the grave on the third day with all power in His hand. Jesus is my Lord and Savior and there is no one like

Him! Thank you for the blood!

LAY ASIDE ALL WEIGHT!

HEBREWS 12:1-2 Therefore we also, since we are surrounded by so great a cloud of witnesses, let us lay aside every weight, and the sin which so easily ensnares us, and let us run with endurance the race that is set before us, looking unto Jesus, the author and finisher of our faith, who for the joy that was set before Him endured the cross, despising the shame, and has sat down at the right hand of the throne of God.

Weight is often a factor when it comes to health problems. Losing weight can help many medical conditions. In fact, the shape of your body and your insides are changed when you lose weight. Most doctors put patients on a fast or a diet prior to conducting tests or surgery. They have discovered that too many variables involved in your weight can interfere in conducting the proper surgery. In fact, too much weight can affect your heart. It can cause heart attacks (cardiac arrest).

In the same way, carrying too much weight emotionally or spiritually can hinder you. The weight of the world, temptation and sin causes people to backslide. They leave Jesus Christ who is their first love for something evil and life threatening. Come back to Jesus Christ, your first love.

In the spiritual sense, so many people are carrying around weights of the world. It could be an old problem, old guilt, or old sin that they should have given to God years ago. Give it to Jesus now! Some people are carrying around the weight of religion and idol worship, when there is no other God but our Father in heaven and His Son, Jesus Christ. Jesus tells us in His word, " Come to Me, all *you* who labor and are heavy laden, and I will give you rest. Take My yoke upon you and learn from Me, for I am gentle and lowly in heart, and you will find rest for your souls (Matthew 11:28-29)." Your faith is because of Jesus Christ. He is the author and finisher of our faith, which is based on the cross of Jesus who sat down at the right hand of the throne of God (Hebrews 12:2). Jesus died on the cross for all people! No one is excluded. God wants you to pick up your cross and carry it, signifying your love for Jesus Christ (Matthew 16:24-25). The enemy roams around like a roaring lion seeking whom he may devour. But God is on your side! He will close the lions and demons mouths because you belong to Him. Call on the name of the Lord, today. We have a cheering section in heaven. The Lord our God is always cheering us on. He also provides us strength for life challenges.

You are a kingdom man and woman. Whatever your circumstance is today, God is looking to see if you will pass the test. He wants to know if you will exercise your faith to remove weights of sin and all that entangle you. We are reminded in this passage that man has no authority to stop you from serving God. Your faith can take you to levels that will blow your mind in Jesus Christ. You must be born again! (John 3:3)

DAY 8

GOD LOOKS AT THE HEART OF MAN

1 Samuel 16:7-8: But the LORD said to Samuel, "Do not look at his appearance or at his physical stature, because I have refused him. For the LORD does not see as man sees; for man looks at the outward appearance, but the LORD looks at the heart. So Jesse called Abinadab, and made him pass before Samuel. And he said, "Neither has the LORD chosen this one."

Make your ministry count! Jesus looks down from heaven to see if you will be obedient to the call to ministry. Jesus even gave the apostles, the prophets, the evangelists, the pastors and teachers, to equip his people for works of service. So that the body of Christ may be built up until we all reach unity in the faith and in the knowledge of the Son of God and become mature, attaining to the whole measure of the fullness of Christ (Ephesians 4:11-13). He is looking at your heart for service and as a witness. God chooses you because you are the best choice for a specific assignment. He knows you're the best because of your heart. God already knows your heart! You can't hide it!

The Bible reminds us that God can search us and examine everything about us. He knows in every household who is right for certain ministries. In Jeremiah 1:5 "God formed us in the womb and He knew you. He knows now and our future before anyone else."

Do you ever get those vibes that people look at you in a certain way? It's crazy, right? They have no clue about the real you. They know nothing about the good heart you have, but some misjudge you. They really do not know your full potential. My friends do not fret. In Samuel 16 "God does not see man the way we see man." God has special insight and knows everything.

When God is choosing, He is looking for a man with the right heart. He knows each of our destinies. When it is all said and done, God knows who will reign in His kingdom in heaven.

When David was being sought after by the Prophet Samuel, God already knew that none of David's brothers would fit the description. Neither of them had the same heart that David had demonstrated before God. God had already chosen David as king and blessed him.

God is looking for you to fill a vital position in his kingdom. God anointed David as king. King David had a tenacity to fight and defeat the enemies of God. Most of all he had a reverent spirit. Allow God to build you up as a man of God after His heart.

I think about building blocks. God builds a little at a time, yet He is effective. God can build man's heart in the same way. I like to think of it like Iron man. His centerpiece appears to be a constructed component in his chest that functions as the heart of his entire power suit. That particular piece is the key to all of his actions in rescuing and fighting. King David's help was God in his heart! God continues to build man piece by piece: heart, mind, soul, body, spirit, and strength. God is the center of our lives for those who believe in Him! Let Him reconstruct you as a man after His own heart. Ask God to be the center of your heart.

GOD EXPECTS AN OBEDIENT SPIRT

ROMAN 5:19-21: For as by one man's disobedience many were made sinners, So, also by one man's obedience many will be made righteous. Moreover the law entered that the offense might abound. But where sin abounds, grace abounds much more, so that as sin reigned in death, even so grace might reign through righteousness to eternal life through Jesus Christ our Lord.

Only God can take your disobedient spirit and change it to obedience; however you have to want to receive it and pray for it. God is the one who changes the heart of man. Even though Adam failed God, the Lord still expressed His love in Adam's family and his life. Sin tries to reign in our lives and the only way to defeat its temptation daily, is to call on the name of Jesus Christ, the Son of God, in prayer.

Adam could have prayed to the Father. Adam could have taken his family to a prayer meeting or fasted. Adam had a responsibility to guard his family. Every man has the same responsibility Adam had. God had made Him in His image and gave him dominion. It was God's order that Adam be obedient and walk in blessings all the days of his life.

Adam is strongest of the two vessels. The woman is the weaker vessel according to 1 Peter 3:7. It does not mean she is not strong. It just means that God created man stronger physically and with more authority. It is easier for disobedience to enter man's heart when the vessel is weak and out of alignment with God. The enemy attacks the man's wife because she is precious to him. Then the enemy attacks the children. The wife needs to remain under his covering in obedience. If she comes from under his covering, confusion and turmoil occurs with an evil spirit leading the way. You want Jesus to lead the way in your life. If you are not careful, the word divorce surfaces from the heart of both or the one that is out of alignment. We remain in alignment with Jesus (John 15). Disobedience is the original reason and cause of sin entering the earth. The first family had stepped off course into disobedience which penalized everyone in creation. Romans 5:14 "Nevertheless death reigned from Adam to Moses, even over those who had not sinned according to the likeness of the transgression of Adam, who is a type of Him who was to come."

Adam was God's first man who was made to walk in obedience; but failed God, our Creator. Thank God for mercy and the power of forgiveness. God had a plan and it was to send His

Son, Jesus Christ who was known as the second Adam. He was obedient to His Father in Heaven. This is also a lesson for all of us. We must as God's children embrace an obedient spirit. Children obey your parents so that your life will be long (Ephesians 6). Parents please teach your children to take this scripture seriously. It is time for parents to take a stand and be parents in truth before God. Teach them about God and his statutes. You can't teach if you don't attend church nor open your Bible. Start today! Be encouraged.

DAY 9

GOD CALLED YOU TO BLESS YOU!

HEBREWS 11:8: By Faith Abraham obeyed when he was called to go out to the place in which he would receive as an inheritance. And he went out, not knowing where he was going.

If you mention to anyone that ten million dollars was awaiting that person in Europe and they had to leave the United States and live there for 3 years and to start a ministry for God in order to receive that 10 million dollars, would they do it?

The Apostle Paul was called to go on several missionary journeys and he answered that call. He answered his call after meeting Jesus on the road to Damascus as a murderer. You have to be able to make up your mind as to who you will listen to and follow. Actually be ready to move out even if profiting is not involved. The logical and only choice should be God.

In a much different scenario, Abraham had been with his family for years. But there was still an inheritance awaiting him by God. When you find yourself staying on the same ground for so many years and no progress has been made, it is time for a change. God always calls us for His purpose and to make a change in your life. God is looking for a man who has ambition, faith and the love of God in his heart. Start moving from that place that hinders you and blocks your blessings. Start looking for a place that God may be leading you.

It is time to put aside things other people spoke about to hold you back. Look to God who has all power in His hand and will bless you in abundance. Our help comes from the Lord. It does not come from man. You might not know exactly where you are going and that is exactly what Abraham experienced when he was called

Abram. There were more experiences God had for Abram to encounter. Then God established a covenant with him. Abram answered God and it led to Him becoming the father of many nations. He became the father of faith! He was a blessed man. When will you obey God? God is calling you, as the man to step out. Your wife may have already asked God for forgiveness and surrendered her heart to Him. What about you?

SOUL WINNERS
SPEAK IT & BELIEVE IT!

ROMANS 10:9-10 that if you confess with your mouth the Lord Jesus and believe in your heart that God has raised Him from the dead, you will be saved. For with the heart one believes unto righteousness, and with the mouth confession is made unto salvation.

Salvation only comes by accepting Jesus into your heart, when you confess it and believe it according to Romans 10:9. Jesus wins souls and change spirits. You have to speak it with your mouth and believe it in your heart. People speak all day long at work and in the house or in a shopping mall. Come Sunday, people are afraid to go up front and just speak and believe their way into God's kingdom. Look at that scripture and see how easy it is to have salvation.

God is multiplying soul winners to go out into the world and tell people about the saving grace of Jesus. Tell them to speak it and believe it. You have to take on that attitude to get results.

These are new disciples going into the world to win people. A soul winner is someone whose focus is on winning people to Jesus Christ, no matter how the enemy opposes or reject them. A soul winner will still take a stand and preach the word for Jesus.

Take a stand for Jesus. Avoid living a double life. We find it so important to have Jesus in your life. Shelia was selling her body as a prostitute after school. She was a living a double life and a lie. These behaviors started before she ran from home and continue until a God Runner intervened in her life. Shelia's heart was hardened against her parents. She starting living as a prostitute, until one day she met Julia at the soup kitchen. Julia joined her at the table where she was eating. Before that, they held a slight conversation as they went through the line. Julia was moved by something she saw in Shelia. Shelia began to open up after Julia asked her why she was there. She explained her rebellion, how she had gotten pregnant at the age of 16 and that her dad had flipped out. Julia explained to her the power of love from Jesus. She also talked about being at peace in Jesus Christ. Some people know exactly how to connect with others to win souls. As angry and full of hate as Shelia had demonstrated earlier, she managed to ask God to take it away. Then she accepted Jesus as Lord and Savior and was received back home by her father. God knows how to move and change hearts.

DAY 10

HIS WILL BE DONE!

Luke 22:42 says, "Father, if it is your will, take this cup away from me; nevertheless not my will, but yours, be done." It was God's will that Jesus continue to the mission of salvation.

If I had to identify the true God Runner, it's Jesus. No one in history has ever done the miracles in ministry that He has done while on this earth as the Son of the Living God. Jesus paid the price for each person. Look at yourself in the mirror and think about you are still alive. He gave His life for each of us. We have access to salvation and our Father in Heaven through Jesus Christ, even those who once rejected Him.

John 1:12-13 states "But as many as received Him, to them He gave the right to become children of God, to those who believe in His name: who were born, not of blood, nor of the will of the flesh, nor of the will of man, but of God.

God wants us to turn our lives over to Him. He can keep us safe. Saints, God wants us to be led by His will. Listen to what Jesus said in His darkest hour in preparation for the cross. He asked the Father if there is another way, take this cup, but only if it be your will. This cup was a crucified death. This would be the only way to salvation. Jesus reminds us of the power that comes from God's will! We must be men of God who allow God's will to lead us on the right path. It requires that we have a surrendered spirit like Jesus displayed to His Father. His sacrifice of physical death was necessary to save God's people. Jesus took on the wrath of God to save every person in the world. Today, make sure you stop by and worship God every Sunday to glorify Him for defeating the enemy for your sin.

KICK THE ENEMY OUT!

LUKE 10:18-23: And He said to them, "I saw Satan fall like lightning from heaven. Behold, I give you the authority to trample on serpents and scorpions, and over all the power of the enemy, and nothing shall by any means hurt you. Nevertheless do not rejoice in this, that the spirits are subject to you, but rather rejoice because your names are written in Heaven." In that hour Jesus rejoiced in the Spirit and said, "I thank you, Father, Lord of heaven and earth, that you have hidden these things from the wise and prudent and revealed them to babes.

God kicked the devil out of heaven so fast it was like a bolt of lightning. What a powerful statement that Luke tells us that Jesus says. "I give you the authority to walk all over those demons in my authority and power." If you belong to Him, you can do just what the scripture states. With authority, kick the demons out of your house and out of your life. These demons mentioned do not have the authority to wreck your life. So stop giving them the authority. Mothers stop allowing your sons to have authority over your house with the demon they bring inside. You allow a gateway to open into your house because you are so into your sons. Mothers, you need to denounce all demons. Get out of your house. Put them under your feet (Ephesian 2).

Luke is talking about demons when he mentions you have authority to trample on serpents and scorpions. These serpents and scorpions are demons. They chase and pursue each man to steal his joy and life. I like what the singing artists, Mary, Mary put in their song, and they sang it well "It's the God in me!" When they sing that song I am reminded that it's not me that does good. Nevertheless, it's the God whose power moves in me and through me. It is God's powers that chase demons off! Jesus loves when you get behind closed doors and fall to your knees and pray because you really go into warfare against principalities. Everybody may not know what you are doing behind closed doors, but God knows. A lot goes on behind closed doors. Speak the word of God "Greater is He in me than he in the world!" You can tell that demon that has been chasing you, that the God in you rebukes all manner of evil. "In the name of Jesus, go back to the depths of hell. Your company is not allowed. I rejoice because His word has kicked you out of my presence, out of my house, out of my life in the matchless name of Jesus Christ."

Lightning can strike some places and leave its marks behind. We usually have vivid memories of those storms that impact our lives. They last for a while and the only way to remove those scars resulting from a storm is through the everlasting power, mercy and grace of our Lord and Redeemer, Jesus Christ. The same God who kicked the devil out of Heaven is the same God who can kick the devil out of your home and out of your life. Every time that enemy attempts to return, you need to open your mouth and speak the Word of God to rebuke it in Jesus name. Speak with authority, "Get thee hence, Satan in the name of in the name of Jesus Christ!"

DAY 11

SAVE YOUR FAMILY FROM THE FLAMES!

Luke 16:19-30 "There was a certain rich man who was clothed in purple and fine linen and fared sumptuously every day. But there was a certain beggar named Lazarus, full of sores, who was laid at his gate, desiring to be fed with the crumbs which fell from the rich man's table. Moreover the dogs came and licked his sores. So it was that the beggar died, and was carried by the angels to Abraham's bosom. The rich man also died and was buried. And being in torments in Hades, he lifted up his eyes and saw Abraham afar off, and Lazarus in his bosom. "Then he cried and said, 'Father Abraham, have mercy on me, and send Lazarus that he may dip the tip of his finger in water and cool my tongue; for I am tormented in this flame.

Have you ever seen a house go up in flames? God is showing us that people can also go up in flames! If you become one of God's you will not destined to those flames. People are self-destructive in so many ways. They allow the enemy to penetrate their minds and hearts. Men, you are to save your family from torment and hell's flames. You have a role to play and a responsibility to help them! Every man should want the best for their families. Do your part as a man and priest of your house. Your goal upfront is to alert your family to receive Jesus as Lord and Savior. Avoid the flames which are where the torment is taking place.

The word torment means an extreme form of human suffering. However, before the suffering, an opportunity exists to get right with God. Lazarus did not have anything, he was poor and hungry.

The rich man was supposed to feed him. Brother, the flames were consuming the rich man because of his failure to show compassion. The rich man needed salvation in Jesus Christ. After he denied Lazarus food, God denied him water to cool the flames.

SECRET PLACE OF THE MOST HIGH

PSALM 91:1-8 He who dwells in the secret place of the Most High, shall abide under the shadow of the Almighty.
I will say of the LORD, "*He is* my refuge and my fortress; My God, in Him I will trust."

Surely, He shall deliver you from the snare of the fowler
***And* from the perilous pestilence.**
He shall cover you with His feathers,
And under His wings you shall take refuge;
His truth *shall be your* shield and buckler.
You shall not be afraid of the terror by night,
***Nor* of the arrow *that* flies by day,**
***Nor* of the pestilence *that* walks in darkness,**
***Nor* of the destruction *that* lays waste at noonday.**

A thousand may fall at your side,
And ten thousand at your right hand;
***But* it shall not come near you.**
Only with your eyes shall you look,
And see the reward of the wicked.

This Psalm is about being secure in our Lord Jesus Christ. He makes everything secure. This secret place is a place that no weapon of the enemy can get through. You can step into a place of security when all hell breaks loose in your life.

Our Father already knows what we need. This Psalm of protection reminds us that our Father in Heaven delivers us from all the tricks and devices of the enemy. God is loving and kind and desires to fulfill your request. Whatever we need, the Father is there. When we get discouraged we do not have to accept anything. We have a God who looks at us from all types of angles. But more importantly, He is the God of a secret place. He is always keeping us secure especially for those who trust him.

DAY 12

HE IS COMING AGAIN

MATTHEW 24: 3-14 Now as He sat on the Mount of Olives, the disciples came to Him privately, saying, "Tell us, when will these things be? And what will be the sign of Your coming, and of the end of the age?" And Jesus answered and said to them: "Take heed that no one deceives you. For many will come in My name, saying, 'I am the Christ,' and will deceive many. And you will hear of wars and rumors of wars. See that you are not troubled; for all these things must come to pass, but the end is not yet. For nation will rise against nation, and kingdom against kingdom. And there will be famines, pestilences, and earthquakes in various places. All these are the beginning of sorrows. "Then they will deliver you up to tribulation and kill you, and you will be hated by all nations for My name's sake. And then many will be offended, will betray one another, and will hate one another. Then many false prophets will rise up and deceive many. And because lawlessness will abound, the love of many will grow cold. But he who endures to the end shall be saved. And this gospel of the kingdom will be preached in all the world as a witness to all the nations, and then the end will come.

This passage explains the many things that will occur before the end of time. These are some of the signs listed above in Matthew 24. Jesus' teaching in Matthew 24 primarily focuses and concerns the future tribulation period and the second coming of Christ at the end of the tribulation. The signs do not affect your salvation. God does not want us to be worried about signs and His return to the earth for those that await Him. You are already saved. It will be a joy to see Him break the sky. It is because those who belong to Him will be caught up in the air in the rapture (1 Thessalonians 4:16). God wants us to continue the good work and witness upon this earth to bring people into His everlasting Kingdom. Saints get out there and win more souls to Jesus. Preach the gospel and nothing but the gospel (Galatians 1:6) under the anointing of the Holy Spirit. Meanwhile do not allow false prophets and teachers who call themselves of God to persuade you in a false gospel or opposite of God's will for your life (Galatians 1:6). If anyone tells you they know the time that Jesus will return, they are trying to deceive you so get away from that lie! Nevertheless, stand firm in the word of God. In fact, do not be ashamed of the gospel because it is the power that brings salvation to everyone who believes. (Romans 1:16) Preach with fire and authority, Jesus Christ, King of Kings and Lord of Lords! Remind people that as Philippians 2:5-10 tells us that at the name of Jesus every knee will bow and every tongue will confess that Jesus is Lord to the glory of the Father in heaven. Make sure you tell them that Jesus loves them with an everlasting love. He died for the world and took away our sin (John 3:16).

Our Lord God of Abraham, Isaac, and Jacob has the power to remove confusion and attacks. Our God is also the God of Moses, Elijah, Elisha, Isaiah and Enoch. He will over power the enemy at every angle in your life. He used these prophets. Jesus will return and we have no need to fret or be worried about it. If you are a kingdom child of God, you are in for the ride of your life. Expect your King Jesus to pick you up. Meanwhile be diligent to preach the word throughout the world. Make an impact by using the gifts of God to discern the false prophets and acting on the ministry God has given you for His glory (1 Corinthians 12). There is nothing you can do about His return, the tribulation period and the signs that will be and are occurring. You just need to stand on the Word of God. Be vigilant in the Word of God.

GOD LOOKS AT MAN'S HEART

1 SAMUEL 16:7 But the Lord said to Samuel, Do not look at his appearance or at his physical stature, because I have refused him. For the Lord does not see as man sees; for man looks at the outward appearance, but the Lord looks at the heart.

Only God has the power to examine a man's heart. Have you had your heart examined by God? He wants to set you on the right path. Let God examine and fix your heart. God has to do it. You do not have that kind of power. He is the only one who can fix it.

God shows us something in the house of Jesse, King David's Father. Jesse had all of sons to pass by Samuel except one, David, the shepherd boy. Jesse could not understand that God was not looking on the outside. Instead He was looking at the heart of a man that loved Him. There is an epidemic of people who have hearts that are not of God. The affects are acts of evil and immorality. God wants your heart so you can belong to Him and receive the blessed life in Jesus Christ.

DAY 13

LOVE YOUR BROTHER

I JOHN 4:20-21 If someone says, I love God and hates his brother, he is a liar, for he who does not love his brother whom he has seen, how can he love God whom he has not seen? And this commandment we have from Him: that he who loves God must love his brother also.

Love is the power of God working through us by touching the lives of others. We are to reveal Jesus Christ in us even when it seems hard to do. Start praying for Jesus to release that love to someone that you may have something against. Love will release to heal every scar and lift the heavy load on your heart, mind and spirit. 1 John 4:8 tells us that "God is love." He wants us to walk in it and live it daily among everybody we meet.

Most people have heard the scripture John 3:16 which states, For God so loved the world that He gave His only begotten Son, that whosoever believes in Him should not perish but have everlasting life. There will always be a circumstance that the enemy will put in your path to try to keep you from loving God and people. The best solution for anyone who experiences these attacks is to stand in the love of Jesus Christ, daily. His love has power to move mountains or anything that seems heavy in your life. Romans 5:5 Now hope does not disappoint, because the love of God has been poured out in our hearts by the Holy Spirit who was given to us. God wants all of us to demonstrate His love by expressing it in our lives, not just lip service in church. Remember love is powerful and it is displayed by action. Love heals, love restores, love changes things. Love can bring families together. Love can reunite and spark marriages. Love puts a flame in the heart. Love is beautiful. Love is on the inside of the heart and manifest outward to others. Love changes a hardened heart. God is Love (1 John 4: 7-12). God is the true love that everyone searches for. Jesus gives us true love every day of our lives. He does not withdraw His love!

PREPARE A TABLE

PSALM 23:5 You prepare a table before me in the presence of my enemies; You anoint my head with oil. My cup runs over.

My Father in heaven prepares a table for His saints in the presence of the enemy. The enemy cannot stop God. God speaks it and ordains it and it's done. Call on his name. Just say "Jesus, you reign on earth and in heaven. You are Alpha and Omega, the beginning and end. You are the one whose blood washed my sin away and now covers me every day of my life. I praise you and worship your righteous name forever. I thank my Father in heaven for your blessings of love and sacrifice. Blessings to your righteous name."

Whenever the Father is in it, you are getting the blessing. When I hear that my cup runs over, it ignites a flame in my heart because I know without a shadow of a doubt in my heart that only God can make my cup overflow. This overflowing cup is the abundance of blessing in Jesus Christ. All kinds of blessing are overflowing in my life because of Him. It is the Father who blesses that way. Every time this scripture is recited, I can't help but to think of the anointing all over me and the call to ministry under His power according to His purpose. Imagine your body soaked in rain. Then God pours out His blessings on your life because of your obedience. It is your season to receive blessings falling on you like rain. Ask God for His blessings. Serve Him with a sincere heart. Tell everyone about Jesus and His goodness. Tell about His unstoppable flow of blessings. His table in one respect represent the fullness of His blessings overflowing in your life. You get filled up at the table by God, nothing else is needed. You feast on what is given to you by the Most High and no one can stop His blessings!

Saints rejoice in His name through dark and troubled times. God walks you through the overflow. He will fill you up with His power to do the purpose set out for you. Then He will get all the glory because it is His! King David was anointed with oil by the Prophet Samuel and His life was filled with overflowing blessings (even in the midst of troubles in his household). God still elevated King David to the throne. He had a heart of repentance. A heart of repentance also connects us to the overflowing blessing in the presence of the enemy. You need to belong to God today. Allow Him to use you so that everybody you know can see the glory of God moving in your life.

DAY 14

GOD IS MY FOUNDATION

2 TIMOTHY 2:19-20 Nevertheless the solid foundation of God stands, having this seal, The Lord knows those who are His, and let everyone who names the name of Christ depart from iniquity.

We have a solid foundation in Christ Jesus. Make a decision today to join the kingdom of God. A father is in the delivery room when his wife gives birth. As she pushes the baby out, the cord is cut by the father. He knows that this is his baby boy or girl. It is the seed that he planted. Now it's a real life for which he is responsible. There is a sense of sealed responsibility and sealed relationship with joy of a newborn baby. Jesus is like that when we are born again. He wants us to know that we are sealed in Him and that He is our solid foundation.

In the Old Testament, Moses was supposed to speak to the rock, but he struck it twice. Nevertheless, most believe that the rock represents Jesus (even in the Old Testament). It was the rock that would provide water for the people. In the New Testament, Jesus is our living water. Jesus is our foundation and our rock. In Matthew 16, the rock is mentioned and called Petra, which means stone. Some reference Peter as the foundation stone for the church, but not the exclusive foundation for the church. The scripture also points to Ephesians 2:19-22 which states, Now therefore ye are no more strangers and foreigners, but fellow citizens with the saints, and of the household of God; And are built upon the foundation of the apostles and prophets, Jesus Christ himself being the chief corner stone; In whom all the building fitly framed together groweth unto an holy temple in the Lord: In whom ye also are builder together for an habitation of God through the Spirit.

Not only is Jesus our foundation, He seals us. No one can break the foundation. No one can break the seal of the Father and His son. Imagine someone trying to take away your son that God gave you. We are sealed in the Spirit of Jesus Christ. He is the head of the church, the foundation and the one who seals us in His spirit. God knows if you are His or not. Make sure you belong to God in His Kingdom.

JESUS IS THE WORD

JOHN 1:1-12 In the beginning was the Word, and the Word was with God, and the Word was God. He was in the beginning with God. All things were made through Him, and without Him nothing was made that was made. In Him was life, and the life was the light of men. And the light shines in the darkness, and the darkness did not comprehend it. There was a man sent from God, whose name *was* John. This man came for a witness, to bear witness of the Light, that all through him might believe. He was not that Light, but *was sent* to bear witness of that Light. That was the true Light which gives light to every man coming into the world. He was in the world, and the world was made through Him, and the world did not know Him. He came to His own, and His own did not receive Him. But as many as received Him, to them He gave the right to become children of God, to those who believe in His name:

Most people ask the simple question that most people want to know. Children are always curious about God. Parents need to be ready to give an answer. Where did Jesus come from? Who is He? In Matthew 16, Peter responds to Jesus by saying, "You are the Son of God." If you believe that He died on the cross and rose from the grave on the third day, then ask Him to forgive you of your sin and come into your heart. Then you will be born again (Romans 10:9). You will be saved and live with God forever in paradise.

Children still want to know where He came from. He was already in the beginning. God is so powerful that He knew exactly what it would take to redeem a dying world. This world was sin sick to the highest degree! It started in the Garden of Eden. God had to send Jesus to fix this sin sickness. Jesus came to be the light of the world so that everyone could be connected to Him and receive this light from God. The same God made it available for you and me. Jesus Christ lives inside of us so that we can have the right to become children of God if we believe in who He is and what he has done. Jesus took on all the sin of the world. He gave us a second chance. Then He made it available for us to receive eternal life. If you ever want to maintain your relationship with Jesus Christ, read the word of God. Open your Bible and read some passages today. Pray and receive blessings in Jesus's name.

DAY 15

HOLY SPIRIT FILLED!

ACTS 2:1- 13 When the Day of Pentecost had fully come, they were all with one accord in one place. And suddenly there came a sound from heaven, as of a rushing mighty wind, and it filled the whole house where they were sitting. Then there appeared to them divided tongues, as of fire, and one sat upon each of them. And they were all filled with the Holy Spirit and began to speak with other tongues, as the Spirit gave them utterance. And there were dwelling in Jerusalem Jews, devout men, from every nation under heaven. And when this sound occurred, the multitude came together, and was confused, because everyone heard them speak in his own language. Then they were all amazed and marveled, saying to one another, "Look are not all these who speak Galileans."

God fills His people in the spirit. He gives power and life to those who worship and celebrate Him! There is nothing else on this planet that must have priority over Jesus Christ as Savior and Lord. The Greek word for Pentecost is pentekostos which means fifty (Dobson et al., 1994). This referred to a Jewish Holiday called the Festival of Weeks. In Leviticus 23:16, the priest is instructed to count seven weeks or fifty days from the end of the Passover to the beginning of the upcoming holiday. The significance of this passage is that the tongues of fire rested on each person who was directed by Jesus to go there and wait.

These followers of Jesus Christ were filled with the spirit and empowered to work the ministry under His authority. The Holy Spirit rested on each person. God wants us to read Acts 2:1-2 to be aware of what He has available for His people.

My question to you is will you choose to worship Jesus Christ in your home and lifestyle? Will you choose to be filled in the Spirit so you can be empowered in Jesus Christ? Or will you allow demon spirits to wreak havoc in your life? Cancel out anything associated with evil including activities like the Mardi Gras in Louisiana. You know there's witchcraft and demons all in the atmosphere. You are to be a Holy Ghost filled person in Jesus Christ. You do not operate in witchcraft, black magic and soothsaying, or demon possessed cults etc. Break every spell by calling on the name of Jesus Christ, the Son of the living God. Ask the Holy Spirit to fill your heart to serve and worship God.

THE HOLY SPIRIT ON MY SIDE!

JOHN 16:5-15: "But now I go away to Him who sent me, and none of you asks me, 'Where are you going?' But because I have said these things to you, sorrow has filled your heart. Nevertheless I tell you the truth. It is to your advantage that I go away; for if I do not go away, the Helper will not come to you; but if I depart, I will send Him to you. And when He has come, He will convict the world of sin, and of righteousness, and of judgment: of sin, because they do not believe in me; of righteousness, because I go to my Father and you see me no more; of judgment, because the ruler of this world is judged. "I still have many things to say to you, but you cannot bear them now. However, when He, the Spirit of truth, has come, He will guide you into all truth; for He will not speak on His own authority, but whatever He hears He will speak; and He will tell you things to come. He will glorify me, for He will take of what is mine and declare it to you. All things that the Father has are mine. Therefore I said that He would take of mine and declare it to you.

God uses each of us as God Runners. We must have the Holy

Spirit teaching, leading, and guiding us in all truth. It is the God Runner that makes a difference with the power of the Holy Spirit inside him.

The Holy Spirit convicts us of sin. God is a personal God. When you become converted after being led by the Holy Spirit, your life is different. You are a believer by faith in Jesus Christ. You become the righteousness of God (Romans 3:22) (2 Corinthians 5:21). You are in right standing with God through the power of the Holy Spirit. God is the God of Judgment. He takes no prisoners! You are either for God or against Him. The Holy Spirit has the power to judge all things. He is God's Spirit among us. The Holy Spirit has already judged the enemies of God. There is a lake of fire for them. You were not born to be an enemy. You were born to be led and sealed by the Holy Spirit of promise and blessings (Ephesians 1:13). The Holy Spirit is about revealing the truth from God and giving God all glory even through His people. God gives us this gift and reveals through the book of Acts what He wants "And when the day of Pentecost was fully come, they were all with one accord in one place. And suddenly there came a sound from heaven as of a rushing mighty wind, and it filled all the house where they were sitting. And there appeared unto them cloven tongues like as of fire, and it sat upon each of them. And they were all filled with the Holy Ghost, and began to speak with other tongues, as the Spirit gave them utterance. And there were dwelling at Jerusalem Jews, devout men, out of every nation under heaven (Acts 2:1-5)."The Holy Spirit is the gift from God. Allow Him to use you for God's glory!

DAY 16

THE MIND OF CHRIST

1 Corinthians 2:16 for who hath known the mind of the Lord, that he may instruct him? but we have the mind of Christ.
Phil 2:5 Let this mind be in you, which was also in Christ Jesus.

Christians are transformed by the renewing of their minds. This is to allow them to take on the mind of Christ. A person with the mind of Christ is someone walking close, hand and hand with the Lord. Their life is no longer the same.

A set mind reveals the character of Jesus Christ and humility (Philippians 2). When you allow your mind to be set by the Holy Spirit, a deeper transformation and blessings occur in your life. Then you can expect to be on the receiving end of blessings. You can also take your new mind in Christ to help others be transformed. In fact, if a Christian is not doing this, he or she is neglecting their Christian duty. We are humble servants of the Most High. In verses 8-10, Jesus humbled himself to the death of the cross. He did it to save a dying world. It was out of committed Love for His Father.

When I first started in the ministry, I set my mind on Jesus first. I also wanted to impress my wife and children by serving God every week in church. I wanted to be a role model for them. I wanted them to see that God had changed me for real. I am still doing the same thing today, preaching to impress God and give Him glory. I want my life to be pleasing in His sight. God is too good not to impress. Set your mind on Jesus no matter what.

We need to always allow God to make our minds like His. We should request Him to refresh our minds when we get off course or need a helping hand. If we have to have a total makeover, so be it. You should desire the mind of Christ, if you desire to operate in His kingdom. Nothing can stop the move of God in your life. However, your mind needs to be open to Him always because wrong thought patterns can block your blessings. He will reflect Himself to others through you. He will reveal things to you in order to bless you. Set your heart and mind on God. Praise and Glorify His name (1 Corinthians 2:1-16).

PEACE IN GOD

PHIL 4:7: and the peace of God, which surpasses all understanding, will guard your hearts and minds through Christ Jesus.

People need peace of mind in everyday life. The way you get the peace you need is by allowing Jesus to come inside your heart and developing a relationship with Him. Make Jesus Christ the center of your life. Where there is no peace, usually there is chaos. We are asked to be peacemakers in Matthew 5. God wants us to have the right attitude toward other people. How are you going to be a peacemaker and you do not have peace yourself? Jesus is our peace. Talk to him every day.

Every man should strive to be a peacemaker. Peace makes everyone in the house happy and joyful and leads to a healthy life.

If the father of the house relaxes, he sets the entire tone in the house. The wife is joyful. His sons and daughters are happy. Life is good!

Man was created to walk in peace. Too many men are searching for peace today. It was lost in the Garden of Eden when sin entered the world. If your life is in an uproar, you can pray for peace. You can walk in peace.

Jesus calmed the raging sea with his disciples on the boat

(Mark 4:35-40). He spoke it and peace was in the atmosphere and the sea. Jesus has all power in His hand. Jesus shows us exactly what God Runners do. They pronounce peace and calmness happens in the atmosphere.

If you are dealing with a child who is running with gangs and smoking drugs, robbing people, and living on the edge, he needs to settle down and get the peace of God in his life. If you are so worried, you as a parent need Jesus in your life so you can get peace. Jesus wants us to know His peace. With peace, our lives, families, churches, and nations can be transformed and revitalized. The peace of God guards your heart. The purpose is to reveal God's love toward us so that we can release love to others. When we have that kind of love usually it signifies that we have absolute peace that comes from God.

DAY 17

FIND GRACE IN GOD'S EYES

GENESIS 6:5-8: Then the LORD saw that the wickedness of man was great in the earth, and that every intent of the thoughts of his heart was only evil continually. And the LORD was sorry that He had made man on the earth, and He was grieved in His heart. So the LORD said, "I will destroy man whom I have created from the face of the earth, man and beast, creeping thing and birds of the air, for I am sorry that I have made them." But Noah found grace in the eyes of the LORD.

God has his eyes on you! He is looking for something unique in every man that represents His glory. Can you imagine how Noah must have felt when God recognized him as a man of grace? Noah's story tells us that God was not pleased with people on this Earth because sin had become rampant in the heart of man. They had allowed sin to penetrate their hearts in every imaginable way. They had the worst imaginations and their minds were constantly thinking evil. In the midst of all of that, God still found a man that He could trust. God found a man called Noah. Noah found grace in the eyes of the Lord, because of his obedience and willingness to listen to the voice of God. That is exactly what believers in the world today should desire. We want to find grace in the eyes of the Lord. Thank God that He has sent Jesus to redeem us. It was Jesus who saw something in us through His Father's eyes.

THE WORD WORKS

HEBREWS 4:12: The word of God is living and powerful, and sharper than any two-edged sword, piercing even to the division of soul and spirit, and of joints and marrow, and is a discerner of the thoughts and intents of the heart.

A God Runner must be equipped. This person runs for God and brings souls into the Kingdom of God. He or she must have the word of God as the sword of life. It is the word that wins souls. I am a witness that the Word works.

Even today in the Armed Forces, swords have specific meanings. A sword is a weapon. The concept causes you to think about fighting. God's word is more powerful than any sword. It has power beyond our imagination. God's word is revelation. It cannot fail.

The word of God is living and more powerful than anything you can imagine in existence. Fortunately for us, the word, which is Jesus, is living in us. It is the word that examines us to see who we really are. It is the word that penetrates our lives. It cuts through sin in us and cleanses us. The Word, Jesus reveals to us who we really are, what we need to do to make a change in our lives. So many people have conditions that they are not even aware of until they visit a hospital. The same thing applies when it comes to needing spiritual deliverance and healing. The word of God will provide it. Jesus proves this through His Word.

If you want to know the power of healing, you need faith and the word of God. Whatever you need in life, the answer is in the word. The word will work out things in your life that you could have never imagined. Ask God to do surgery on you. He is able to change your identity with His word. He can do anything but fail. He is all-powerful.

It was the word of God in the beginning that created the world. When God spoke whatever He spoke, the universe came into existence. All power is in the word of God. In John 1, the Bible describes Jesus as the word. The scripture reads in John 1:1-2 In the beginning was the Word and the Word was with God, and the Word was God. The same was in the beginning with God. John tells us who is the word, where the word came from, and who is with Him. The Word will have much impact in the life of the believer.

DAY 18

THE SPIRIT FILLS US WITH POWER

Acts 2:4: And they were all filled with the Holy Spirit and began to speak with other tongues, as the Spirit gave them utterance.

A God Runner must be filled by the Holy Spirit. He has to be able to discern other spirits. A God Runner uses those gifts that God gave him (1Corinthians 12, 13,14). The God runner can speak God's word and use the gifts that God gave him/her. A God Runner is not limited because he or she is a child of the Most High God whom the Holy Spirit works through.

God enables us to speak with authority because of his Holy Spirit. Speaking in tongues is evidence that a person is filled and influenced by the Holy Ghost (Acts 2:8). You also received the Holy Spirit at the time you received Jesus Christ, even if you did not speak tongues at that moment (Romans 10:9-10). Jesus, His Father and the Holy Spirit are one. When we repent and are baptized in the name of Jesus for forgiveness of our sin, we receive the gift of the Holy Spirit (Acts2:38). Because we are filled with the Holy Spirit, we speak God's word with authority and power and as a result people are saved. Peter preached and about 3000 people were saved (Acts 2:41). Jesus speaks to the storm and tells it "peace be still." He does it because He is filled in the Spirit to say the least. He is the only begotten Son of God.

The tongue has the power of life and death (Proverbs 18:21). This is to inspire someone who may have a calling to serve God. "Lord, thank you for filling me with the Holy Spirit. My life has not been the same since you saved me and filled me. I pray that the power of your word is manifested throughout the earth for your purpose."

FAITH IN JESUS!

HEBREWS 11:1-3 Now faith is the substance of things hoped for, the evidence of things not seen. For by it the elders obtained a good testimony. By faith we understand that the worlds were framed by the word of God, so that the things, which are seen, were not made of things that are visible.

The God Runner falls in this super hero category. The God Runner is someone with unwavering faith. The God Runner serves God and has the power to help all people get delivered and receive a breakthrough in Jesus Christ. The God Runner has faith that he can bring souls to Jesus. The God Runner has everything and more like the Avenger characters below. Will you become a God Runner today? Listen, faith in Jesus Christ is the key ingredient!

Every year a film producer produces a new Avengers, Batman, Superman or Captain American movie. As old as I am, I still get those wonderful feelings of excitement from heroic acts in those movies. One week I am the Man of Steel. The next week I am Iron Man. I just can't make up my mind which one I want to be for sure, maybe all of them. They are fun to watch because of two primary reasons; one they show the ultimate confidence and faith. Secondly they always get the victory by saving lives and defeating the enemy. I always remember seeing Superman stopping the fastest locomotive by flying to the front and pushing it in the opposite direction or just lifting it with shear strength. I have had some of the wildest thoughts about super heroes. What if they all got together, the Dark Knight, Superman, Super Friends, Spider Man, the Incredible Hulk, Flash, Green Hornet, Hercules, the Transformers, the men of 300, and my new character that I invented, The Transformation Man, in a big production movie to save the world. I hope someday these movies reflect on superheroes bringing people to salvation. This is the job of the

Transformation Man. The Transformation Man is part preacher and part superhero. Their actions can have a positive impact on the Christian world as well as secular groups.

Faith gets God's attention because you depend on Him. God reminds us that the worlds were formed by faith. A man with faith steps into the supernatural and walks under the Holy Ghost's influence. Use your faith now! God can do all of what every super hero can do and more. Jesus has defeated that old enemy! Every Christian is supposed to walk stronger each day like an Avenger. Take back your house! Take back your heart! Take by your dignity! Take back your mind! Take back whatever the enemy stole from you. Take everything back because you belong to God. You have to take it back and step into your destiny and victory with God. You are a faith fighter and a man of God.

When the saints come together, they can take back the city. It's because Saints are God Runners in Jesus Christ. They have the anointing on their lives. Imagine the power God placed in you! Today, you can tell all of your friends, relatives and your wife that you are a man of Faith. You can step out on faith when God calls you, like Abraham did. Faith is a weapon itself. Not only do you have faith, but Jesus has faith and is at the right hand of the Father in heaven. When the Holy Spirit goes to the Father on your behalf, His faith is unleashed and God blesses you. Keep activating your faith within. Turn your faith up every day to get a new victory. In Jesus name, Amen.

DAY 19

THOUGH HE SLAY ME, I TRUST HIM

JOB 13:13-15: Why do I take my flesh in my teeth, and put my life in my hands? Though He slay me, yet will I trust Him. Even so, I will defend my own ways before Him. He also shall be my salvation, for a hypocrite could not come before Him.

No matter what happens in your life, put your trust in God. People will let you down. That is a guarantee because they are human. Whenever fear and terror approach, Trust God regardless. God will remove the fear and terror in your life. That terror is the enemy trying to eat at your soul.

Job expresses that regardless of the pain and suffering or how bad life can get, he still needs God in his life to heal him, comfort him and restore his life. It starts with trusting God and believing in Him to take care of life's difficulties. Regardless of who we are, we still get tested and experience trials. The question is - will you pass the test even when the heat is turned up?

Trust is essential in every relationship. If you do not show trust to your wife, you can lose her. In each marriage, the wife and husband trust each other to make the relationship work and last for life. Trust is believing in one another; and most of all believing in God. God wants us to trust Him. Tell the Lord that you will trust Him in all things.

The enemy specializes in trying to rob God's people of joy, faith and peace. It looked like Job had every reason to turn his back on God. Job should have given up on life with all the damages going on in his family life and his personal pain. The enemy was using Job's wife to try to make him stop trusting God. His wife told him to curse God and die. That was an awful thing to tell your husband, but that's how the enemy works. He gets at the man through his wife. However, if that man has God in his life, no devil in hell can conquer him, because he belongs to Jesus, the son of the living God.

Don't allow fear and a hard blow run you away from God. Life deals us blows. It can seem impossible to handle at times. But God is there in the midst of your confusion, fear and doubt. God is there to help reinstate your faith in spite of your crisis. He will pick you up, hold you up, and restore your blessings as long as you believe in Him and trust Him.

HE RESTORES LIFE

EZEKIEL 37:4 Again He said to me, Prophesy to these bones, say to them, O dry bones, hear the word of the Lord!

God strategically places us as Christians in places to wake up people that are walking dead. He uses the anointing on our lives. He wants to quicken those that have given up on Jesus or fell by the wayside and even those who are allowing the devil to run rampant in their lives. Do you have anyone in your family who is like these dead bones? They are just lying there waiting for someone to give them the word of life! When you deliver the word of God, it is life to anyone who hears it. It's time for you to restore your family and friends. You need to take authority. Invite them to a revival even after you give them a scripture, every day. Watch the new life come inside of them. God is speaking to you today and giving you the authority and a new challenge in life. Are your family members' lives worth saving today? Then do it! Give them a word from God! Stop waiting and procrastinating. Is your grandchild's life worth saving? Is your friends' life worth saving? If you do not make the effort when God has called you to help them, then you have been disobedient to God and they may die in that valley. Those dead bones will stay dead and decay. If you decide to be obedient to God and speak a word of God in their lives, they will live and pass on multiple blessings to more than a thousand times a thousand for generations to come. This is because you obeyed God and showed the love of God and cared for other people and your household.

You can take the initiative to do it! In this case, the Lord specifically told Ezekiel to prophesy over dead bones. God put His anointing on Ezekiel to speak life into the dead bones. Let us take a look at the power of God through Ezekiel's mission.

The Lord told Ezekiel to speak over an army of dead bones to raise them up (Ezekiel 37). This is super faith and an anointing of God. Can you see the picture? Here lies an entire nation of dead bones in front of you. God's power is flowing through your words to speak and the bones return to life.

God wants men, women and children to be restored back to life and back to Him. God will bring whatever He wants back to life. If it is dead, God is able to restore. Lazarus was dead and Jesus called him back to life (John 11:38-44). A little girl was dead and Jesus brought her back to life. Elijah used his anointing to bring a little boy back to life (1King 17:17-22). God has the power to bring people back to life. He will use you in the ministry. That is correct, you! We, as Christians, believe in the resurrection of Jesus from the dead. God raised Him up and defeated death. God is showing us what He can do with anyone who needs to be restored back to life. The Centurion Soldier asked Jesus to just speak the word and his servant would be healed. This soldier showed great faith in the eyes of Jesus. Jesus restored the servant (Matthew 8).

God may have sent you to that church so that the pastor can prophesy over your life. He preached restoration and your life was restored. You know it because God has given you twice as much as what you lost! You know it because God is using you to be fruitful in multiple ways. You are now a fruit bearer that brings people back to life. You can bring a drug addict back to life! You have an anointing to help restore people in Jesus Christ. You can help a prostitute give her old life up, receive and follow Jesus. You can help bring high school drop-outs back to school and back to Jesus. You can help deliver a runaway and destructive youth back to his or her parents. You can inspire a gang member, gang leader, and pimps to turn to Jesus. In your assignment as a God Runner, you help bring people of all ages and issues to receive Jesus Christ as Lord and Savior. You are a spiritual mentor. You have the infilling of the Holy Spirit inside of you! You help to develop other people for the purpose of Jesus Christ. You are a kingdom restorer. Go and get them for God's Kingdom!

DENY YOURSELF AND TAKE UP YOUR CROSS

MATTHEW 16:24-27 Then Jesus said to His disciples, "If anyone desires to come after Me, let him deny himself, and take up his cross, and follow Me. For whoever desires to save his life will lose it, but whoever loses his life for My sake will find it. For what profit is it to a man if he gains the whole world, and loses his own soul? Or what will a man give in exchange for his soul? For the Son of Man will come in the glory of His Father with His angels, and then He will reward each according to his works.

This is exactly what a God runner does. The God runner denies himself and picks up his cross to follow Jesus. Will you become a God Runner today? Look at Jesus on the cross for the entire world.

It is a huge blessing to deny yourself for Jesus Christ. You need to understand the level of demons that will hate you. The name of Jesus makes demons tremble. Nevertheless, there is good in denying yourself for Jesus. One of the perfect examples is the Apostle Paul. When he met Jesus, he left everything behind to preach Jesus. His goal was to become a church planter, Christian changer, global church mover, and soul winner. He became the kind of witness Jesus was looking for. It was the same Jesus who knocked him off of his beast and transformed him forever. He lived for Jesus Christ. He wrote two thirds of the gospel because the spirit of the Lord touched him so deeply. You might need a deep touch, today. If you are still off the path, God can reach you wherever you are. Drugs can't stop him, legions of demons can't stop him, hatred can't stop him, and no other power has the ability to stop him. He is the sovereign and omnipotent, God. He is all powerful. He is the mighty God. There is no one like Him.

Deny yourself and follow Jesus. What is denying yourself? It means to give up. Crucify the flesh. Count on God for everything. The Holy Spirit will carry you over.

Elisha was another one who had left what he was doing and walked under the teaching of Elijah through God. Because of his obedience and willingness to serve God, he received the mantle from Elijah and a double portion of the power God granted him. It takes a true follower in obedience and faith to get a double portion. He can bless in the doubles and move mountains in the doubles. He is the God of double portions. Ask God today to help you by the power of the Holy Spirit to pick up your cross. Ask Him for a double portion in the area you want to give him glory in. It's your time now. Put all selfishness aside and serve God the rest of your life. Give Him glory! Watch how your family benefits.

DAY 20

JESUS IS THE WORD

JOHN 1:1-12: In the beginning was the Word, and the Word was with God, and the Word was God. He was in the beginning with God. All things were made through Him, and without Him nothing was made that was made. In Him was life, and the life was the light of men. And the light shines in the darkness, and the darkness did not comprehend it. There was a man sent from God, whose name was John. This man came for a witness, to bear witness of the Light, that all through him might believe. He was not that Light, but was sent to bear witness of that Light. That was the true Light, which gives light to every man coming into the world. He was in the world, and the world was made through Him, and the world did not know Him. He came to His own, and His own did not receive Him. But as many as received Him, to them He gave the right to become children of God, to those who believe in His name:

The Word has been illuminated to me on all of my preaching occasions. God's word is like a lamp that comes on and allows you to see what you could not see in the darkness. I learn more and more about Jesus as the years go by. It is because the Holy Spirit illuminates the word of God. This passage is so powerful because it tells us that Jesus is the word of God. It was 1994, when the word was illuminated to me. I saw God, clearly. Every time I study the word of God, I can see Jesus as the light of the world. This happened as I had just found my way back to God. He knows exactly how to reveal himself to each of us. As the Pastor was teaching this in Massachusetts in 1994, it came alive in front of my very eyes. The light was turned on. When the light was turned on inside of me, it changed me. The light is still working in my heart and spirit to this day.

John makes it perfectly clear that Jesus is the Word. Not only is He the Word, everything was made by the Word of God. It made sense to me because Jesus is the light. When he reveals Himself, he uses His light. He is the light of the world so that people can see Him in His word and a manifestation of His power. People can see Jesus in His saints. Amen. I received Jesus and begin to preach the gospel. I was telling everyone about Jesus. Today, I so glad to be a God Runner to tell everyone about Jesus and that He saves, heals and delivers.

RAISED UP IN CHRIST!

ROMANS 6:1-8: What shall we say, then? Shall we go on sinning so that grace may increase? By no means! We died to sin; how can we live in it any longer? Or don't you know that all of us who were baptized into Christ Jesus were baptized into his death? We were therefore buried with him through baptism into death in order that, just as Christ was raised from the dead through the glory of the Father, we too may live a new life. If we have been united with him like this in his death, we will certainly also be united with him in his resurrection. For we know that our old self was crucified with him so that the body of sin might be done away with, that we should no longer be slaves to sin because anyone who has died has been freed from sin. Now if we died with Christ, we believe that we will also live with him.

Recently, I started back on a routine of exercise for a few days. I wrote a note to my wife. I told her that I would be our trainer. I made a list of what we should do. The list included 3 sets of pushups, 3 sets of sit-ups/crunches and 20 minutes of running. The sit-ups work on the stomach so I can get a wash board effect for my wife. Every time I did a sit-up, I thought about the power that I was developing in my body to make me a fit person. Each time I did a sit-up, something was happening. I was gaining more and more power. My goal was to become a new man, inside and out. Nevertheless, physical fitness alone is not the answer. There also has to be spiritual fitness and its starts with believing and agreeing in Jesus Christ.

God has so much amazing power in every facet of life; every measurement of life, and in every imaginable way. Truly His design of life is in us as His creation. God, our Father, has the blueprint of creation in His hand and all that are made by Him. The scripture above reminds us that we are partakers of the resurrection because we believe that He died and rose from the grave. The believer shows the world their faith in the resurrection, by their baptism, because it symbolizes the death, burial and resurrection. Each baptism candidate steps into the water and then is immersed into the water and raised up. This new convert or believer rises to a new life.

DAY 21

HE IS RISEN!

MATTHEW 28: 1-8 Now after the Sabbath, as the first day of the week began to dawn, Mary Magdalene and the other Mary came to see the tomb. And behold, there was a great earthquake, for an angel of the Lord descended from heaven, and came and rolled back the stone from the door, and sat on it. His countenance was like lightning, and his clothing as white as snow. And the guards shook for fear of him, and became like dead men. But the angel answered and said to the women, "Do not be afraid, for I know that you seek Jesus who was crucified. He is not here; for He is risen, as He said. Come, see the place where the Lord lay. And go quickly and tell His disciples that He is risen from the dead, and indeed He is going before you into Galilee; there you will see Him. Behold, I have told you." So they went out quickly from the tomb with fear and great joy, and ran to bring His disciples word.

Jesus is raised from the dead and proof is in the Word, the old grave and the shroud of Turin. Death was defeated by Jesus Christ. The entire scientific team that studied the shroud of Turin has absolutely, positively proven that the body of Jesus was erected by a miraculous power into the depths.

Only God could have rolled the stone away and raised Jesus up. Imagine stepping inside the tomb and witnessing God raising Jesus up from the dead. Keep that thought! That thought alone will transform you and make you a believer in Jesus Christ. It's so powerful to know that it happened.

Today, Jesus is reminding us that we have stones in our lives that need to be moved by the power of Jesus. He already removed the sin that was entangling you and me. We need to have Jesus in our lives to remove stones that keep rolling back in place. We need to be serious about God. We need Jesus to remove the stones of hatred, jealousy, disobedience, pride, and lack of love. We need to have a free spirit to worship Him in the beauty of His Holiness. Jesus desires that we be set free. There is nothing too hard for God to roll back from your life. He rolled back death and Jesus rose from the dead. He lives in heaven and his eyes are on everyone full of love and joy and power.

GOD SET YOU FREE!

EXODUS 12:12-16 "For I will pass through the land of Egypt on that night, and will strike all the firstborn in the land of Egypt, both man and beast; and against all the gods of Egypt I will execute judgment: I am the LORD. Now the blood shall be a sign for you on the houses where you are. And when I see the blood, I will pass over you; and the plague shall not be on you to destroy you when I strike the land of Egypt. 'So this day shall be to you a memorial; and you shall keep it as a feast to the LORD throughout your generations. You shall keep it as a feast by an everlasting ordinance. Seven days you shall eat unleavened bread. On the first day you shall remove leaven from your houses. For whoever eats leavened bread from the first day until the seventh day, that person shall be cut off from Israel. On the first day there shall be a holy convocation, and on the seventh day there shall be a holy convocation for you. No manner of work shall be done on them; but that which everyone must eat that only may be prepared by you.

The blood would protect anyone who was covered by it. A pure lamb's blood had to be on the doorpost of the house so that the destroyer would pass over those who obeyed God. When God expressed His judgment, then and only then, would the breaking point be revealed in Pharaoh. God dealt Pharaoh one last chance. Pharaoh had such a hardened heart, so hard that even after God took his first-born, he still didn't want to be in the will of God. You would think that life was precious to Pharaoh since he was a ruler. But evidently, he did not care and relied on his evil spirit and self-interest. Pharaoh sent his army to chase God's people in the desert. God revealed two more miracles to Pharaoh. He made a whirlwind of fire to block the army from God's people and the Red Sea. Moses held the rod up and the sea opened and the people walked through to the other side. Pharaoh's army went into the Red Sea and God closed the sea on his army. It was finally then when Pharaoh was convinced that God is God. Moses' God is God and there is no other like Him. God can set you and I free from our Egypt.

DAY 22

DREAMS OF BLESSINGS

GEN 45:3- 13: Then Joseph said to his brothers, "I am Joseph; does my father still live?" But his brothers could not answer him, for they were dismayed in his presence. And Joseph said to his brothers, "Please come near to me." So they came near. Then he said: "I am Joseph your brother, whom you sold into Egypt. But now, do not therefore be grieved or angry with yourselves because you sold me here; for God sent me before you to preserve life. For these two years the famine has been in the land, and there are still five years in which there will be neither plowing nor harvesting. And God sent me before you to preserve posterity for you in the earth, and to save your lives by a great deliverance. So now it was not you who sent me here, but God; and He has made me a father to Pharaoh, and lord of all his house, and a ruler throughout all the land of Egypt. "Hurry and go up to my father, and say to him, 'thus says your son Joseph: "God has made me lord of all Egypt; come down to me, do not tarry.

As a result of Joseph's dreams, he was able to preserve life. God gave him dreams to bless his family and all of Egypt. The power is also in the fact that Joseph was an obedient servant to God. He also knew that he had a relationship with God and that resentment to his brother would only hold back the blessings that God had in store.

Dreams from God are on a total different level than ordinary dreams. I believe God will reveal His dreams to you if they are from Him. You must be careful not to get it twisted. You need to talk to God about all dreams. In Joseph's case, his dreams are of future blessings over his family and Egypt and even the ruler.

Joseph had a relationship with God. It is important that everyone knows that. Dreams open your mind to see things in the future. God reveals these dreams. He reveals a great deal of what He expects and already has purposed for your life. What is your dream about? Today is your day to speak it back to God and see if it was from God. Joseph knew about his. Sit down start writing your dream, mission, desires, goals and/or purpose in life even if God did not give it to you yet. Write it down and ask Him for it. He can either approve it or deny it. God's will covers all things. Nothing is beyond God. He will answer you. Do not answer for God. Seek ye first the Kingdom of God and all other things will follow (Matthew 6:33).

It is important that you start seeing yourself in the very moment of that dream. Do you remember Joseph? Joseph was the son of Jacob who had 12 sons. Joseph was betrayed by his brothers, cast into prison, and taunted by Pharaoh's wife to have sexual relationships. Prior to having all the troubles in life, Joseph had a dream that his brothers and family members would bow before him someday. He had a dream that He would be in a high position of authority granted by God's power. He became the second highest in command of Egypt. It was a dream and it was the favor of God. God sent Joseph into Egypt to preserve life. One dream can move a nation of people, kings and rulers of the world.

God gave Joseph the wisdom to store up goods through the famine. Although Joseph had powerful dreams and interpreted other's dreams, he was still a man of God in action for the Lord. Are you a man in action for the Lord? Or are you just idle? He backed up his words. God is looking for men who are dreamers, yet can also back up their words through action.

DON'T LOSE YOUR OWN SOUL!

MATTHEW 16:26: For what profit is it to a man if he gains the whole world, and loses his own soul? Or what will a man give in exchange for his soul?

Gamblers put everything into winning a huge pot or prize. They are willing take a chance at it. Some win, some lose. The question becomes what are you really winning? If you prefer anything over Jesus, you have already lost. But you still have a chance to get it right!

I am always reminded of Olympians and how they put everything in it to win the gold medal. Their profit is a gold medal, fortune, and fame. They could have been putting their all in all into the spreading the word of God. If you are going to be an Olympian, you should put God first. When you win your gold medal, let everyone know that God helped you. We should put God first in our lives. Make sure we give Him the glory.

You can ask almost anyone if they would love being a millionaire or billionaire. The obvious answer is yes! Microsoft and Apple are leading the computer industry in businesses that are valued in the millions and billions. We live in a world where everything revolves around profits and people wanting to get rich quick. You can increase earnings and profits using various strategies. However, do not allow greed to slip in and become the focus in your heart instead of Jesus. A greedy heart can destroy your life with your entire family and friends. You see profits can be made in every ministry, every business, and in the market place. What makes a man work so hard to get money? It is his desire to get ahead in life and gain recognition beyond his competitors. Don't lose your soul to gain the whole world. Don't allow greed to get the best of you. Balance life and riches and most importantly, put on Jesus Christ and make Him a priority. Jesus's disciples made a conscience decision that they were going to follow Him (Mark 12). Jesus called them His disciples because they submitted to His authority, teaching and practiced His teachings. Some even wrote the Bible to reflect His words. These men knew what would be their profit. The gain is life in Christ Jesus. Money does not win souls; Jesus wins souls through His word, spirit and power. He is the only God and there is not one like Him! Give Him glory! Your life is the best life in Jesus Christ rather than in any other profit.

DAY 23

THE POWER OF TRANSFORMATION

MATTHEW 17:1-9: Now after six days Jesus took Peter, James, and John his brother, led them up on a high mountain by themselves; and He was transfigured before them. His face shone like the sun, and His clothes became as white as the light. And behold, Moses and Elijah appeared to them, talking with Him. Then Peter answered and said to Jesus, "Lord, it is good for us to be here; if you wish, let us make here three tabernacles: one for you, one for Moses, and one for Elijah." While he was still speaking, behold, a bright cloud overshadowed them; and suddenly a voice came out of the cloud, saying, "This is my beloved Son, in whom I am well pleased. Hear Him!" And when the disciples heard it, they fell on their faces and were greatly afraid. But Jesus came and touched them and said, "Arise, and do not be afraid." When they had lifted up their eyes, they saw no one but Jesus only. Now as they came down from the mountain, Jesus commanded them, saying, "Tell the vision to no one until the Son of Man is risen from the dead."

What if you saw an octopus in the ocean transform right in front of you? What if you actually saw the butterfly transform from a caterpillar to a butterfly with wings, taking his first flight? What would go through your mind? I would probably say to myself, look at God! The power of transformation is so marvelous that it can leave one speechless.

Peter, James and John were with Jesus at the transfiguration. The transfiguration suggests a transformation not only outside, but inside, as well. First of all, He had to give them something to see in order to witness to the world. Jesus reveals His glory to His disciples in the mountain. At the same time, He presents two other witnesses of God's divine power, who were prophets from the Old Testament. Moses may have been mentioned because he was caught up to God in His glory. Elijah was one who was caught up to heaven without dying. His picture represents the rapture (1 Thessalonian 4:13-18). It seems that the Lord is expressing that He was pleased with His son, Jesus. He was pleased with His son for various reasons. Jesus is the fulfilment of the Old Testament, the prophets and the law. He also became an obedient witness on earth and His Father could bear witness to it. Jesus also proved to show love that is superior to any man on earth. Jesus walked in the glory of His Father on earth and never sinned. He expressed His Father's will, love, and performed miracles of restoring people's lives. The Lord was expressing the power of witnessing through His chosen prophets of the past, Moses and Elijah. Nevertheless, His emphasis was definitely on the Son of God who did not hesitate to come to earth and fulfill his mission for His Father and become the sacrifice to save the world from God's wrath.

God wants His people to know that as they become transformed, they will also be pleasing in God's sight until He returns. God wants His people to allow the Holy Spirit to take root like that transformation power in that butterfly so that each Christian can take flight in this world and tell the whole world about Jesus.

WORSHIP GOD ONLY!

REVELATION 4: 10-12: the twenty-four elders fall down before Him who sits on the throne and worship Him who lives forever and ever, and cast their crowns before the throne, saying: " You are worthy, O Lord, To receive glory and honor and power; For You created all things, And by Your will they

exist and were created."

One of the most amazing and blessed scenes in the Bible is these elders casting their crowns before the throne of our Lord to show blessings, honor, glory, worship, and praise unto the most High God.

Every man must make it a priority to bow down every day to the living God. Let Him know that you are serious about your relationship. This picture of the 24 elders giving honor and glory to God in the heavens is impacting. Take a moment and think on this scene of worship. God is all powerful and full of blessings. He alone blesses us daily. It is then that they understand His majesty and desire to bow down and worship Him. "The twenty four elders fall down before Him. They cast their crown before the throne, saying you are worthy O' Lord, to receive glory and honor and power." They recognized that he had created all things including that very moment of glory. They cast their crowns to show complete submission, worship, reverence and exaltation to Him. God deserves the praise. He is God and the one who holds my soul in His hand. Worship to you O Lord! You are magnified and given all glory forever and ever through eternity. Get ready to worship God when you turn your life over to Jesus. Tell some people you know how He blessed you!

DAY 24

MAN UNDER GOD'S INFLUENCE

EPHESIANS 5:17-19: Therefore do not be unwise, but understand what the will of the Lord is. And do not be drunk with wine, in which is dissipation; but be filled with the Spirit, speaking to one another in psalms and hymns and spiritual songs, singing and making melody in your heart to the Lord,

The wine was given as stated in the book of Timothy to help heal stomach aches and other illnesses. Jesus does not want you to get it wrong and think it's okay to drink and get drunk. Drunkenness alters your mental state. You are capable of being completely destructive in your home as well as on the highway. Alcohol makes you become belligerent and can cause you to become sexually vulnerable to women. Some people will get drunk and never know what dangers they caused themselves and others. Some people have gotten drunk and conceived children. It is wrong to become intoxicated. How can you be ready for Jesus if you are drunk? It also causes you to operate under the influence of a substance rather than the influence of the Holy Spirit. If you love God, you will change this habit and behavior. Times have changed and people do not care about you trying to impress them with drinking. Stop telling yourself that you need a drink. Instead tell yourself that you need to be filled with the Spirit and under His anointing. God wants our lives to be influenced by Him daily!

THE CROSS

JOHN 19:31-35: Therefore, because it was the Preparation Day, that the bodies should not remain on the cross on the Sabbath (for that Sabbath was a high day), the Jews asked Pilate that their legs might be broken, and that they might be taken away. Then the soldiers came and broke the legs of the first and of the other who was crucified with Him. But when they came to Jesus and saw that He was already dead, they did not break His legs. But one of the soldiers pierced His side with a spear, and immediately blood and water came out. And he who has seen has testified, and his testimony is true; and he knows that he is telling the truth, so that you may believe

This was the greatest act of love that man has ever known. Jesus's sacrificial act of love on the cross is demonstrative of His extreme selflessness and blessings for mankind. The soldiers pierced His side and blood and water came out. According to most scholars, this represented washing (by the blood) and cleansing power (by the water). This is why my mother cried when all her children were baptized. She was touched by His grace, love and tender mercies in church. Not only should mothers influence their children, the man of the house (priest) should make sure his children know the basics of being a Christian. Help them read and learn these scriptures such as Mark 1, Luke 1, 2, Romans 10:9-10, John 3:1-10, 1 Corinthians 13, Galatians 5, John 19 and Mark 16. The movie "The Passion of the Christ" was a remarkable depiction of Jesus giving His life for our sin (Isaiah 53:1-7).

I still did not understand it all. Resurrection Day - this was the day that love was demonstrated beyond measure. No other event in history can compare. This is the most critical event that could have ever taken place on earth. This is why every preacher is to preach the cross, grave, and resurrection. The blood of Jesus washed you and me whiter than snow. He took our wrath (Isaiah Chapters 53:1-7). In verse 7, the word of God says, He was oppressed, and he was afflicted, yet he opened not his mouth: he is brought as a lamb to the slaughter, and as a sheep before her shearers is dumb, so he openeth not his mouth (Isaiah 53:7). We should pick up our cross daily because of our Lord and Savior (Matthew 16:22-25).

Saints, if it had not been for the Lord on our side where would we be? We would have had to experience the wrath of God. He died for you and me.

DAY 25

BIND IT AND LOOSE IT

MATTHEW 18:18 "Assuredly, I say to you, whatever you bind on earth will be bound in heaven, and whatever you loose on earth will be loosed in heaven.

Binding means simply forbid it. Loosing it means to allow it. You must use your authority to forbid the enemy to put its hands on your children. Loosing also means to set something free from; it also means a breakthrough. For example, a breakthrough can occur from a bad habit of dealing with drugs in your life. You can be loosed from it. Jesus removed demons from a man who was cutting and hurting himself. He was in bondage. Legions operate to try to destroy you. This man probably would have killed himself. Jesus loosed him from demons! If it had not been for the Lord, he would have been dead. This is exactly why God makes God Runners. These God Runners are the kind of men and women who will not settle for demons to defeat you and me. Jesus has defeated them! God Runners settle only for a Holy Ghost Party. In other words they are demon destroyers. They loose people in the name of Jesus. They are God's priests, anointed ones. They are precious in God's sight! You need to hurry up to church or find a nearby anointed minister of the Lord and choose salvation, right now! Also ask him to help you get loosed from the grip of the enemy. You need help, now! Stop trying to do it yourself!

When people can't do it themselves, God will send someone to help you. God sent Jonah to a city called Nineveh to tell the people to repent so God could restore the city instead of destroying it because of sin. Jonah initially went the opposite direction in disobedience God. God intervened using a whale to swallow Jonah so he could experience hell temporarily. Jonah realized as he spent time in that whales belly that his life and purpose belongs to God. He finally went and preached to the city repentance and God blessed him and the city. They praised God! God has the power to take entire cities out of bondage. He can definitely bind spirits that are in your life.

It is your time to start binding those demons, so you can move ahead in life. Repent of your sin to Jesus. Then ask God to loose you so you can walk in forgiveness. Jesus is saying bind it now. Deal with the issues of your personal life. Your inner man needs to be free. If you have been in an abusive relationship, pray and ask God to bind that spirit of abuse. Ask God to restore you completely with the mind of Christ.

What is holding you down and possessing your life? Break away from it in the name of Jesus. Break away from homosexuality and immoral behaviors, Break from relationships of lust. Turn to the living God and be born again. Ask Him to loose you from any sinful lifestyle. God has restored you if you believe in Him and walk in newness of life.

CALL ON JESUS!

Romans 10:13-14 For whosoever shall call upon the name of the Lord shall be saved. How then shall they call on him in whom they have not believed? and how shall they believe in him of whom they have not heard? and how shall they hear without a preacher?

In this passage, the Apostle Paul informs the reader to call on the name of Jesus for salvation. However, you must believe when you call on Him. Accept Him as Lord and Savior. You heard of people being born again. Jesus saves! He heals! He restores! He gives life! In His name, anything can be accomplished. This is your hands down opportunity to step into the Kingdom of God. This goes for you and everyone in your household.

I heard just the other day about a young boy who prayed for his father, who was lost for years. It got to a point that his father was placed in a senior citizen's home. After 30 years had passed and just a few days before the boy's father had passed away, the care provider who looked after the boy's father called him and gave him some exciting news. His Father had accepted Jesus Christ into his heart after years of praying for his father. The power of prayer works. There is plenty of evidence in the Bible. Give an invitation to your family member to accept Jesus into their hearts. You can read it to them now. You can also help them go to the front of the church to accept Jesus when the preacher finishes the sermon. Don't be afraid, it's easy! It takes about 30 seconds. Read Romans 10:9 which is one of my favorite passages: "That if thou shalt confess with thy mouth the Lord Jesus, and shalt believe in thine heart that God hath raised him from the dead, thou shalt be saved" You can call on the name of Jesus, because all power is in His name. There is no other name that has power. You see Jesus is Lord and Savior. He has all authority in the world. Not only does He have all power, but He gives us power, just like He gave to His disciples. They spread the good news of salvation. They also shared that Jesus is the Son of God who died on the cross and rose from the grave with all power.

DAY 26

WHEN GOD OPENS YOUR EYES

2 KINGS 6:16-17 And Elisha prayed, and said, "LORD, I pray, open his eyes that he may see." Then the LORD opened the eyes of the young man, and he saw. And behold, the mountain was full of horses and chariots of fire all around Elisha. So when the Syrians came down to him, Elisha prayed to the LORD, and said, "Strike this people, I pray, with blindness." And He struck them with blindness according to the word of Elisha.

Elisha was one of God's runners. He was a prophet that spoke according to the will of God. It's powerful when you have a prophet around you that God has anointed to speak a word through prayer.

When God opens your eyes, get ready for miracles you have never seen. You can see what's in front of you and all around you. Your discerning nature kicks in.

God wants your eyes open so that you can see the enemy for yourself and know that God will fight you battles. You have the victory. It's your time to start seeing your blessings from God. Whenever, you need God to show you something, ask Him to open your eyes. Allow God to help you to see in the spirit realm. Don't feel defeated or walk with fear another day, because God is on your side. No weapon formed against you will prosper.

The promises of the Lord are for you. God has blessings laid up in heaven, waiting on you. You no longer have to wait on anyone to make you feel of value and worth. You are a child of the Most High! Do what Elisha did when the enemy came his way. Elisha prayed to the Lord to open their eyes. When you pray, the Lord will show you things that you can only see in the spirit realm. He showed the young man His armies for His support. God can open eyes in any kind of situation.

Elisha did something else remarkable in his combat situation. He asked the Lord to strike the enemy with blindness and the Lord did. Oftentimes people allow the enemy to afflict them with blindness, disease, hurt, shame, and guilt. There are so many things that keep them in bondage. If they could learn to call on the name of Jesus and ask Him to strike the enemy and believe that God can and will. Then their faith would increase and confidence in God would manifest in their lives in a greater way. Ask God to strike the enemy with a bolt of lightning just like he was kicked out of Heaven to Hell. Lord, if you could just get the enemy off of the back of your people, they could start witnessing to the lost. Keep him away from my family and my wife and my children, I will serve you. Keep my faith determined and true to you, Lord.

A FIGHTING SPIRIT

JUDGES 7:4-8 But the LORD said to Gideon, "The people *are* still *too* many; bring them down to the water, and I will test them for you there. Then it will be, *that* of whom I say to you, 'This one shall go with you,' the same shall go with you; and of whomever I say to you, 'This one shall not go with you,' the same shall not go." So he brought the people down to the water. And the LORD said to Gideon, "Everyone who laps from the water with his tongue, as a dog laps, you shall set apart by himself; likewise everyone who gets down on his knees to drink." ⁶ And the number of those who lapped, *putting* their hand to their mouth, was three hundred men; but all the rest of the people got down on their knees to drink water. Then the LORD said to Gideon, "By the three hundred men who lapped I will save you, and deliver the Midianites into your hand. Let all the *other* people go, every man to his place." So the people took provisions and their trumpets in their hands. And he sent away all *the rest of* Israel, every man to his tent, and retained those three hundred men. Now the camp of Midian was below him in the valley.

Here is another God Runner. When God prepares you to be a God Runner, look out enemy. The anointing of God is coming your way. Jesus will always have the victory. It's His way or the highway. Devil, you have to go in the name of Jesus Christ, the Son of the living God.

Your wars and battles are already won! Jesus is on your side. God's selection is powerful. Every year the military is sending off more than 20,000 soldiers to fight battles somewhere in this world to maintain peace and democracy. Simply put, soldiers are heroes. They are deployed to save lives and restore freedoms to nations all around the globe. So often they are in places like Africa, Korea, Germany, Russia, Afghanistan, or Iraq.

War could break out at any time. Soldiers have to train to be ready for the call of duty. In spite of fear, they have to be equipped and ready. In that same way, you have to be prepared for battle and get into the heat of it with God on your side. God was not about to allow the Midianites to keep Israel in oppression. Seven years of oppression was already too long (Judges 6). Gideon was a humble Soldier and leader who answered the call of God on his life. Gideon was known for asking God to make dew on a fleece on dry ground, and also the opposite; to make the ground with dew and the fleece dry. God proved His power both times. To prepare for war, Gideon followed the instruction of God to reduce his army to 300 men from the original 32,000 men to fight the Midianites (Judges 7). God still allowed the Midianites to fight with 135,000 Soldiers. Do not allow fear to overtake you. God has you covered all around regardless of what it looks like. All of God's Soldiers on the battlefield and in the Armed Forces need to develop a prayer life, now, more than ever. Pray to the Lord in Heaven and thank Him for His love and kindness. He will deliver according to His will and purpose. Believing in the power of prayer is crucial. It is prayer that will hold things together. Prayer will save the soul. Prayer will deliver and help your spirit. Prayer will lift you up every time, if you trust in Jesus. Prayer is your access to Jesus and for Him to dispatch your assigned angel. Pray for protection like in **Psalms 91:11. God said, "I will give my angels charge over you, to keep you in all your ways.** What a blessing to know that God will do this holy thing for you and me. God also expects His people to put on the whole Armor of

God for protection and warfare (Ephesian 6:10-18). Christians have power to intervene in warfare.

We also need to pray to protect our troops from defeat. All of the saints should be praying to protect the thousands of soldiers that are deployed. Pray for peace and to strengthen every family and the countries involved. Praise Him because of His grace, mercy, blessings, protection and the victory in Jesus Christ.

DAY 27

PLANTED BY RIVERS OF WATER

Psalm 1:1-3 Blessed is the man who walks not in the counsel of the ungodly, Nor stands in the path of sinners, Nor sits in the seat of the scornful; But his delight is in the law of the Lord, And in His law he meditates day and night. He shall be like a tree planted by the rivers of water, That brings forth its fruit in its season, Whose leaf shall also not wither; And whatever he does shall prosper.

The Lord is the one who plants and blesses to produce fruit in due season and according to His will and purpose for our lives. A blessed man reveals who he is in Jesus Christ. When people are around him and come in to contact with him, they will know that he is planted in God. When you are planted in God, blessings flow. People recognize you as a blessed man.

God notices immediately the obedience in a man and that causes God to bless him even more. This is a man who has the word of God inside of him. He is full of the seed of God. God is the one who brings forth the fruit using you (which is the tree planted by the rivers of water). God operates through us in the abundance.

God is looking for men that will receive the blessing and remain (John 15) on course in planting His word and His love all around the world. Be fruitful for Jesus so someone can receive the blessings. When He gave the command to the apostles in Matthew 28, it was a commission, a charge to spread the word and bless people throughout the world. His intent was to execute every word in Matthew 28. Jesus wanted His apostles then and His witnesses today to plant and watch the fruit multiply. This comes as you preach and teach and baptize in the name of the Father, Son and Holy Spirit. He wants men that will stay on the path of obedience and servant hood. He wants us to stay the course even when it gets difficult. Stand firm in the power of God's word when challenges and difficulties occur. We need to maintain a positive and steadfast attitude in this walk.

We are on a mission for Christ to bless others. We stand against all evil by the power of prayer and faith in Jesus Christ. We are fervent prayer warriors. We are under the influence of the Holy Spirit to express fervent and effectual prayers. We pray because as God sent an angel to Daniel during His prayer, so can He send angels to attend to our prayers. We pray just as Jesus prayed to the Father in the Garden, "Not my will, but your will be done".

Then we plant when we pray because he hears us. We plant seeds of hope and encouragement. We plant a seed so someone will accept Him as Lord and Savior. We plant the word of God to receive a harvest. Let us not be weary in doing good, for in a proper time we will reap a harvest if we do not give up (Galatians 6:9). The God Runner is a harvest chaser! He or she brings people in multiples to Jesus Christ because they don't give up. The God Runner is committed to Jesus.

We can also get a breakthrough when we pray as people of God. We stand on the word of God and His promises to answer prayer and send the power of breakthrough and fruitfulness.

A BLESSED MAN PLANTED IN JESUS CHRIST

Psalm 1:1-3 Blessed is the man who walks not in the counsel of the ungodly, Nor stands in the path of sinners, Nor sits in the seat of the scornful; But his delight is in the law of the Lord, And in His law he meditates day and night. He shall be like a tree planted by the rivers of water, That brings forth its fruit in its season, Whose leaf shall also not wither; And whatever he does shall prosper.

Make a new goal in life to plant yourself in Jesus Christ. If you are not born again, go to Jesus right now! Turn your life over to Him. The Bible in John 3:3 says "You must be born again." When you accept Jesus as Lord and Savior, get deeply rooted in Him. Often people get planted and deeply rooted in ungodly things that lead to destruction and the enemy holds them captive. Avoid alcohol and drugs homosexuality, prostitution, fornication, orgies and adultery. Break all of those demonic strongholds that manipulate your life. In other words, don't start something that will destroy your life. Those things are demon controlled spirits so break them in the name of Jesus Christ.

The Lord desires you to plant for him and be fruitful in His Kingdom according to His perfect will. Obeying His word is one of His highest orders because it proves to Him that the word is planted in you. You are walking with God's seed inside of you. When He blesses, He makes the rivers flow. Rivers of water that flow in your life will continue in abundance because God wants to bless you in abundance.

God is looking for God Runners who will preach this to those that are living an ungodly lifestyle. The God Runner is the one who denies himself for Jesus Christ. God is looking for men who will receive the blessing and stay the course. We need to hang in there regardless of what things look like. Deception comes in all forms to trick saints and those that are lost. The enemy strives to deceive. He is a loser, a liar, and has no authority over you. You are blessed and highly favored of God. You are fruitful. You bear fruit in the name of Jesus Christ. You reign in Christ.

DAY 28

POWER IN THE TONGUE

James 3:8-10 But no man can tame the tongue. It is an unruly evil, full of deadly poison. With it we bless our God and Father, and with it we curse men. Who have been made in the similitude of God. Out of the same mouth proceed blessings and cursings. My brethren these things ought not be so.

God spoke blessings when He had finished making all things in creation and they were pleasing in His sight. God spoke and life began. Heaven and earth were filled with all kinds of blessings. Everything that came out of God's mouth was pleasing to Him and For His glorious purpose. God revealed His identity to us through the words He spoke. He reminds us of our destiny to walk in His word. We were made to speak blessings and not curse one another. He gave us these tongues for the proper use. The tongue is an instrument to be used for God's glory and edification. The tongue is powerful and carries the word of God and the word of God is more powerful than a two- edged sword that pierces even the very asunder of the soul (Hebrews 4:11). The word also tells us in Proverbs that the tongue has the power of life and death, and those who love it will eat its fruit (Proverbs 18:21). In that same chapter, the scripture also tells us "the words of the mouth are deep waters, but the fountain of wisdom is a rushing stream. It is not good to be partial to the wicked and so deprive the innocent of justice. The lips of fools bring them strife, and their mouths invite a beating. The mouths of fools are their undoing, and their lips are a snare to their very lives (Proverb 18:4-7).

Acts 2:4 speaks of tongues of fire during the day of Pentecost, it says, "And they were all filled with the Holy Spirit and began to speak with other tongues, as the spirit gave them utterance." God wants us to know that He was revealing Himself to show us what He did in the book of Acts by allowing the power of tongues to rest on His people. God has no respect of person. No one is above Him.

He will empower all His people for the uplifting of His Kingdom. He poured out the Holy Spirit on people then and is doing it today as well. The Holy Spirit will work on behalf of the Father in all circumstances.

When the tongues of fire rested on them, they spoke with power. They did not speak hate; they spoke edification to the Lord. They spoke in different languages, but all languages in the form of edifying God. It was the Holy Spirit that was the guiding power enabling these people to get their blessing. He is the controller on God's behalf.

God can do anything with the tongue. He can use it for His glory. Speak the word with your tongue. 1 Corinthians 12:10 and 14:1-22 tells us to speak prayers using your tongue. Bless someone today with words coming from your lips and tongue. Bless people with your tongue.

God will purify your hearts to help us to speak according to our identity in Christ Jesus. People will know us by the way we speak. God is not asking us to be perfect, but He is asking us to change our ways. God is completely aware of our strengths and weaknesses. Our Lord Jesus desires that we speak blessings in the lives of other people rather than curses.

ACCESS TO GRACE

Ephesians 2:8 For by grace you have been saved through faith, and that not of yourselves, it is the gift of God.

How often do you have access to something in your life? Actually we have access to doors in our homes. If we can't get in the front door, panic just might set in. We have access to the car that we drive daily. We have access to the engine in that car by using a key to start it up so it can be used for its purpose of transportation. These are blessings and for the most part things we need in our lives to go about our daily routines. Some are necessities in our lives. The gift is salvation. Access to grace is powerful because God allows us to use faith for grace and salvation. We have eternal life in Jesus Christ because of our faith in the power of His grace.

Everyone has access to grace.

Grace is a gift from God. It is the key source of strength for salvation through faith. Most people are still unaware of the power in grace. You must keep faith at the center. It is grace that keeps you from committing both natural and spiritual suicide. Grace is unmerited favor given by God. No one can earn grace. It is not a power source that you turn on and off. No one can work for grace. It is freely given. Jesus gives us grace. Jesus came with grace and truth that all men might believe and be saved into His kingdom. We never had a right to this blessed gift of grace from our Lord. Our penalty was simply death. We were destined to the wrath of God. But He washed us as white as snow in the power of His love.

When someone is truly saved, they have the ability to understand God's holy blessing called grace. They can see the evidence of it in their lives. Even as a new creature in Christ, they can see basically all good things in life associated with His grace. The scales have fallen off. It is by the grace of God that we all live day to day, breathe moment to moment, and love time again

We deserved God's wrath because of our sin nature. Nevertheless, in grace, He took away our sin that we may live according to His perfect will and love each other. In grace, there is also favor that is beyond man's ability. Grace never turns its back on you. Grace never ceases to bless your life. Grace has the perfect mix of God's love to sustain you and help you to grow all together. We are speaking of God who is all powerful and sovereign. He is the God who spoke the universe into existence. He is the God you as a believer have access to each and every day of your life. Give God praise and glory in Jesus name!

DAY 29

SEED EXPERIENCE

LUKE 8:10-12 And He said, to you it has been given to know the mysteries of the kingdom of God, but to the rest it is given in parables, that seeing they may not see, And hearing they may not understand. Now the parable is this: The seed is the word of God. Those by the wayside are the ones who hear; then the devil comes and takes away the word out of their hearts, lest they should believe and be saved.

Seed is all around us and inside of almost everything. Every child is a product of a seed of a man in this world. This man is considered to be your biological father. God equipped man with such a blessing to produce on this earth with some woman in mind. I found it so interesting that a woman will protect that seed –child from birth until death. It is one of the most remarkable things that I have ever noticed in society. It is because seed has power in it. One seed can alter a woman's body and life forever. Lord, I feel the anointing on that statement. Don't ever let anything steal your seed.

Farmers are protective of their land and live-stock. One reason is because there is power in the fertilized land. That means it's receptive to the seed that will be planted. When an enemy comes against them, there is usually a battle that will take place.

There is power in the fertilizer and seed that makes the process of production and bearing fruit in vineyards work. No one knows the exact process which causes the seed to produce and make a harvest.

Joseph's story is a blessing because it reminds us of God's abundance when we store up for a season. Jesus wants us to understand that the word of God is the seed. When we read the word the enemy wants to steal it and cause us to stop believing. But the Bible says that there is power in the word and you can stand on it. .

God teaches us the law of sowing seed. When you become a seed sower, you might as well get ready for the enemy to put forth his best tactics to steal the word from your heart. You are a threat to the enemy. He will come after you with all his might to take that seed from you. You become a target because of the word of God inside your heart. Once the enemy thinks that he has stolen the word from your heart then he wants your mind and your confession to be destroyed as well.

The enemy will try to hinder, steal, and conceal your blessings, every time. The enemy is concerned about taking everything you own, including your family. You are like fertile ground that receives new seed. The enemy does not want the word (seed) in your heart, your mind and in your spirit man. Once you get the word rooted inside you, then you can walk in the fruit of the spirit and be filled in faith. You can walk under the anointing and nothing can stop you.

The enemy's mission is to take the seed from you, stunt the seed in you, burn it up, choke it out of you, and utterly destroy it. This devil does not want the seed to take root. If it does not take root and it will not produce. Your seed takes root and produces children. My Father's seed took root inside my mother and now you can see me! The big picture is that I am my father's seed and now I am a minster of Jesus Christ speaking and delivering His seed, which is the word of God. The devil does not play fair and certainly has no respect for you or the seed. This is real warfare. You and I need to use prayer as a weapon. Every Christian must embrace the power of the Holy Spirit's protection. Start recognizing the actions of the Holy Spirit to protect your life. In Psalm 91, God gives His angels charge over us to protect us.

Believers have to have the Lord's power for their faith walk. It helps to be cautious in the walk. Don't give in to foolish demands of others. Do not be persuaded to do worldly things unpleasant to God. God sees all things. He wants us to walk in obedience. He even plants His seed in us to demonstrate His power within us. God wants us to stir the gift in us by faith and serve Him. Give your life to Jesus Christ, today. You have waited long enough. Today you may be able to help someone who has fallen to by the wayside.

THE VISIONARY MAN

Habakkuk 2:2-3 Then the LORD answered me and said: "Write the vision and make *it* plain on tablets, that he may run who reads it. For the vision *is* yet for an appointed time; But at the end it will speak, and it will not lie. Though it tarries, wait for it; because it will surely come, it will not tarry.

Think about movie and film makers, they have a vision of what kind of movie they want to make. They can see each scene.

When God gives you a vision, you are already equipped in the spirit. Use your gift to write your vision and make it plain to yourself and anyone around you.

You may have to give up something to make your vision happen. You may have to work hard at some things. So be strong in the Lord and in the power of His might. Remember, if the Lord is in it, then it will be successful. Your visions come from God. He is the maker of your inner being and your entire mind. Seek Him for clearer visions. Make your request known to God. You have some visions and dreams inside that must be awakened and manifested to give Him glory.

Write the vision and make it plain. You see things that God has for you as clear as day. Don't refuse the blessing that God has for you. Start speaking it in your spirit that you will be obedient to our Father in heaven. Start confessing with your lips the promises that God has for you. You do not have to rely on someone else to announce it. Just call on Jesus, the Son of the living God. God will bless your vision, especially if it is for His kingdom. If you want it, get it. Blessings are for the taking from the Lord. Blessings will overflow in what you do for the Lord as long as you glorify Him.

There are many men who built churches for the uplifting of God's Kingdom. They are built to worship and praise God. King David had a vision to build a temple for God and to place the Ark of the Covenant inside. King David could not build the temple because he had blood on his hands. The Temple had to be built by his son Solomon. You see God has the vision over man. God is looking for those who will be obedient and act on the vision He gives.

When Moses saw the burning bush, his heart was ignited to move toward God. Nevertheless, He moved toward the mountain and discovered it was the voice and the presence of the Lord with a mission for Him. God blessed Moses that day and for days to come. He empowered Moses so that he could tell Pharaoh to let His people go. You see God had a plan for His people. They were to be set free from bondage and prosper all their days.

Jesus had a vision and made it plain. His vision was to lay down His life for the world. His vision was to take away the sins of the world. Jesus made it plain that He was the Savior of the world. His vision was to cover everyone in His precious blood. For God so love the world that He gave His only begotten Son for whosoever believeth in Him shall not perish but have everlasting life (St. John 3:16). This vision that God has for us is for an appointed time. Jesus' death, burial, and resurrection were for an appointed time. All praise to His holy and righteous name.

DAY 30

THE LAST TRUMPET

I COR 15:52 in a moment, in the twinkling of an eye, at the last trumpet. For the trumpet will sound, and the dead will be raised incorruptible, and we shall be changed.

The Lord our God is giving us a chance to get ready because it will happen fast. We will not be given another warning after this one. The trumpet will sound and God is in motion. Just that fast God's saints will be changed, as He tells us, "in a twinkling of an eye." We will put off all the old man. The spirit of the living God will be in us and we will be like Him! No corruption, no old flesh, no old ways. The Bible makes it clear that we will be changed by His power.

The Lord reminds us that we are here today; but tomorrow or any moment Jesus could break the sky. Are you ready to be with the Lord on that great day?

Have you ever had something in your life that hit you so fast that you did not know it was coming? Lightning is one of those occurrences that happens in the blink of an eye. There are other things that you do not expect to happen that come and you do not expect it in the spirit realm. We don't worry about it because some things cannot be explained by humans. In the case of Jesus, we just trust that He will return and the believer will be caught up in the air to meet Him. We should trust that God will do what He says, just as we trust our hearts to beat every day. We do not question whether or not our hearts will continue to pump blood every day. We just know that it will beat and we will keep living. There are people who do not understand that God allows their heart to beat.

BREAK EVERY STRONGHOLDS

2 CORINTHIANS 10:4-5 The weapons we fight with are not the weapons of the world. On the contrary, they have divine power to demolish strongholds. We demolish arguments and every pretension that sets itself up against the knowledge of God, and we take captive every thought to make it obedient to Christ.

God wants us to break every stronghold and chain in our lives. God's power can take out any stronghold, any demon spirit, anything that comes up against Him and His Saints. I still can't get over the display of power God used when Elijah called on Him through prayer against Baal, idols and false gods (1 Kings 18). God can break every Jezebel and demonic stronghold in your life with His power. He may use someone with an Elijah Spirit in faith and prayer (1 Kings 18:37-39). Most people remain in their stronghold because they think like the rest of the world and give in to the enemy. Use your faith to come out of strongholds. Call on the name of Jesus to break every stronghold that is on your life. Sexual lust is usually the biggest stronghold. Sexual issues, as well as drug addictions and other problems are devices of the enemy. God wants you to speak that you are more than a conqueror in Jesus Christ. This will motivate and encourage you. You were born to think in the spirit and exalt our Lord Jesus Christ. God wants you to get everything in the right gear and make something happen.

Start shifting it to make a difference in this world. Somebody needs you to encourage them and to help them overcome things that have held them back. It is your time to walk in freedom and in the abundance of God's blessings. Always remember when God has something good ahead for you, the enemy is hiding in the trench ready to ambush you and to take away the goods that the Lord has given you. Hold on to your faith in Jesus. He will keep you under His perfect protection and care. He will anoint you to get His mission completed which involves lifting up others that have been put in shackles by the evil one. Speak to the chain and loose those shackles. Be strong in the Lord and the power of His might. Break every stronghold that the enemy throws at you. You are a born again, sanctified believer and child of the most High God.

DAY 31

PREACH JESUS WITH POWER

2 CORINTHIANS 4:5-12 For we do not preach ourselves, but Jesus Christ as Lord, and ourselves as your servants for Jesus' sake. For God, who said, "Let light shine out of darkness," made His light shine in our hearts to give us the light of the knowledge of the glory of God in the face of Jesus Christ. But we have this treasure in jars of clay to show that this all-surpassing power is from God and not from us. We are hard pressed on every side, but not crushed; perplexed, but not in despair; persecuted, but not abandoned; struck down, but not destroyed. Always carry around in our body the death of Jesus, so that the life of Jesus may also be revealed in our body. For we who are alive are always being given over to death for Jesus' sake, so that his life may be revealed in our mortal body. So then, death is at work in us, but life is at work in you.

The light switch came on when I was called to ministry. The light came on so that I can preach Jesus as Lord. Jesus had placed treasure inside of me to preach His name! The treasure in this vessel is the power, light and message of salvation in Jesus Christ. God knows that when we preach Jesus, the light shines through dark places in the lives of all people. We preach Jesus so people are delivered from persecution, darkness, being crushed, and from all attacks of the enemy that try to bring us down. When we preach Jesus, life and deliverance is at work in us because of His all surpassing power.

God wants us to be ready and qualified! When I first read the qualification of a deacon and a bishop in 1 Timothy 3, I thought about the strictness and the holy life that an apostle and man of God have to live for service in Jesus Christ. I read the importance of God setting the qualifications for man to serve in obedience to Jesus Christ. When he has truly received the power of Jesus inside of him, he will serve. It made me think about Moses and the Ten

Commandments that God gave him for people to live by. Can a man truly live by this standard in his appointed position? The answer is yes. He may not be able to live the law out. But that is why God gave us grace and the Holy Ghost. But he definitely can live out those qualifications, as long as he entrusts the Holy Spirit for strength and obedience. It is only the Holy Spirit's guidance that will see us through all of God's standards. God sent Jesus to fulfill the law. We can't do it on our own. Remember, all things are possible by God. At the same time, He put them there because He knows our potential strengths and weaknesses. He also wants us to rely on His power, not our own. He put things in place to maintain order and the love of God displayed in our lives.

DON'T GIVE IN TO THE DEVIL

EPHESIANS 4:25-27 Therefore each of you must put off falsehood and speak truthfully to your neighbor, for we are all members of one body. "In your anger do not sin": Do not let the sun go down while you are still angry, and do not give the devil a foothold.

This scripture is powerful because the Apostle tells us something that is so needed. Love is needed not anything false. Don't give in to the devil by any means. You have to be able to witness to your neighbor therefore your realness counts.

You can start by expressing love every day from the moment you wake up in the morning. Tell your wife you love her and give a kiss that she will remember. Show her you know how to kiss. Then set a romantic date. You start your date with honesty, realness and love. The intent is to help the love move to a higher level. Keep your marriage strong. If you allow the devil to come into your house and shake up everything, then you will see for yourself what he is capable of destroying. If you really don't want it to get that far, you can stop his manipulations and lies in its tracks. Faith in Jesus Christ must be activated. Jesus will stop it for you. Do not give that devil an inch. Glorify Jesus in everything you do, today. That is how you get your house back in order. Start praying daily a simple prayer. Lord, I love you and need your helping hand in every situation of my life. Lord, I worship and praise your name forever, in Jesus name. Then you can watch all of those demons flee at the name of Jesus.

You need to speak with power. The enemy has strategies to infiltrate your home and your body, mind, and spirit. He comes from every angle to destroy you and your family. Take a stand in Jesus name against the devil using the word of God. Let the word of God be spoken from your mouth. Use your tongue to confess the word and the power in it. Speak Psalm 27, The Lord is my light and my salvation whom shall I fear. The Lord is the strength of my life.

DAY 32

HE OPENS DOORS TO BLESS YOU

REV 3:7-11 "To the angel of the church in Philadelphia write: These are the words of him who is holy and true, who holds the key of David. What he opens no one can shut, and what he shuts no one can open. I know your deeds. See, I have placed before you an open door that no one can shut. I know that you have little strength, yet you have kept my word and have not denied my name. I will make those who are of the synagogue of Satan, who claim to be Jews though they are not, but are liars—I will make them come and fall down at your feet and acknowledge that I have loved you. Since you have kept my command to endure patiently, I will also keep you from the hour of trial that is going to come upon the whole world to test those who live on the earth. I am coming soon. Hold on to what you have, so that no one will take your crown.

A door is vital for every home and building. The door is in most cases the first thing that people notice about a structure. Whether it is beautiful or it lacks the best taste, doors attract people. There is always something behind closed doors. Business deals are made behind closed doors. We end up behind closed doors each day of our lives. You go behind closed doors for privacy, security and a need for personal space. In a home, there are many doors. How much time do you spend behind closed doors? The Lord talks much about doors. No man can open doors for you that God has closed. No man can close doors that God has opened for you. Blessings are associated with doors. The good thing about all the doors is that when God opens doors, no one can shut them. No one can make deals with God behind any door. There are those closed doors that are designed to stunt your spiritual growth. But God has an open door for those that call on His name and believe in Him. There is nothing too hard for God. When God puts things in order for you to prosper, no doors can shut you out. When God wants you to succeed in a business plan that He gave you to layout the vision and goals, nothing can stop you. Instead all doors have to open because of the Lord's favor and blessings on your life.

REIGNING KING OF KINGS

REV 11:15 The seventh angel sounded his trumpet, and there were loud voices in heaven, which said: "The kingdom of the world has become the kingdom of our Lord and of his Christ, and he will reign for ever and ever."

A king's crown gives him a distinguished look above everyone else. He is set apart as the king of that land. We are kings as well ever since we crossed over into salvation, accepting Jesus as Lord. Jesus is the reigning King in my life and in the entire world. He is identified by everyone who sees the crown on his head as King of Kings and Lord of Lords.

Some crowns may be locked up in museums for display as a part of history. The crowns of kings of old had precious stones, gems, and diamonds. Many were made of gold and eloquently shaped perfectly to fit the head of a designated king. Some of those crowns were very distinguished. When David was ruler of Israel and all the land, General Joab would bring crowns to King David so that he could know that the victory had been taken from those heathen kings.

As saints of Jesus Christ, we have a heavenly crown that we focus on, while on this earth. We witness to the lost souls and bring them into the Kingdom of God. You see Jesus has already washed us whiter than snow. We have been washed in the blood of the Lamb! God Runner, tell everyone you know that a crown in heaven awaits you because you have kept the faith in Jesus Christ and you belong to Him. Because you are one of Jesus' children, you will reign with Him forever. Just think on that fact: we will reign with Jesus! There no place I would rather be than in His love and reigning with Him. My friend read the book of Revelations. I guarantee you that you will never be the same in your heart.

THE POWER TO DRIVE DEMONS OUT
LET GO TODAY!

MARK 16:9 When Jesus rose early on the first day of the week, he appeared first to Mary Magdalene, out of whom he had driven seven demons. She went and told those who had been with him and who were mourning and weeping. When they heard that Jesus was alive and that she had seen him, they did not believe it.

Jesus drove demons out of Mary Magdalene. Don't allow anything to possess you. Ask Jesus to drive the demons out and anything else that's not good. Those spirits will try to get inside of your heart. They want to hold you back from serving the Most High God. Drive them out in the name of Jesus Christ.

In Mark 5:2-4, Jesus cast demons out. "When He got out of the boat, immediately a man from the tombs with an unclean spirit met Him, and he had his dwelling among the tombs. And no one was able to bind him anymore, even with a chain; he had often been bound with shackles and chains, and the chains had been torn apart by him and the shackles broken in pieces, and no one was strong enough to subdue him. It took Jesus to drive these demons out who were legions (thousands). Matthew 8:28-33 tells us "When He came to the other side into the country of the Gadarenes, two men who were demon-possessed met Him as they were coming out of the tombs. They were so extremely violent that no one could pass by that way. And they cried out, saying, What business do we have with each other, Son of God? Have You come here to torment us before the time?" Now there was a herd of many swine feeding at a distance from them. The demons began to entreat Him, saying, "If You are going to cast us out, send us into the herd of swine." And He said to them, "Go!" And they came out and went into the swine, and the whole herd rushed down the steep bank into the sea and perished in the waters.

Those demons illustrate a spirit and act of suicide. My point is - if you are trying to drive anything out, you best call on Jesus name. Jesus drove those demons out of those men to set them free. Let every demon go out of your life today, in the name of Jesus. Jesus has power over all things and nothing is impossible for Him! Consider, when God shows up, deliverance happens because His power goes forth (Exodus 14:31). Whatever you are going through, ask God to show up and restore your life and give you deliverance. Call on the name of Jesus Christ, the Son of the living God!

DAY 33

FIX YOUR EYES ON GOD

2 CHRONICLES 20:11-12 See how they are repaying us by coming to drive us out of the possession you gave us as an inheritance. O our God, will you not judge them? For we have no power to face this vast army that is attacking us. We do not know what to do, but our eyes are upon you."

You will never go wrong when you put your eyes on Jesus. Make Him the center of your life. Make Him the focus each and every day. King Jehoshaphat's Army was being surrounded and perhaps overrun in so many ways. King Jehoshaphat had the best idea of the day. Call upon the Lord in prayer for everything, especially in a time of war. Can you imagine what would happen if general officers and enlisted men and women of the Armed Forces of every branch called upon the name of the Lord? God would respond to all sincere requests because He is God and He holds to His word. God hears your prayer every time you pray. He hears the battle cry and the distress call in your prayer. King Jehoshaphat spoke these word, "We do not know what to do, but our eyes are upon you" This sounds like a plea and at the same time a total submission to God to deal with the circumstances of war and all troubles involved and around it.

God has ways of blessing His people. Have you ever had a bully that was just ready to take you out and you knew that the bully was going to win. That is exactly how Satan works. He bullies people. God has an Army so big that nothing can stop Him. In one blink, He can summon every angel and some to come at your request and take out all the demons in hell and those around you. In response to King Jehoshaphat's prayer, He made it clear to "be not discouraged, for the battle is not yours, but God's." The Army at this point had only one responsibility, stand still and watch the mighty hand of God work in this battle. He will resolve all things according to His power and authority. He showed His tender mercies toward King Jehoshaphat and his Army. The King only needed to obey God. God wants us to keep our eyes on Him! Victory belongs to our God.

I was listening to special concerning race relations. Race issues in America are like a constant cancer that stirs up hate and wars. Racism is behind wrongful deaths and a divided America. A famous basketball star visited a Baltimore Town Hall meeting with angry African Americans inside a church. The tension was so deep and the pain was engrained into the minds of those who lost love ones. There was a heavy sense of being terrorized and victimized due to racist acts against them. God made me think in this scripture when King Jehoshaphat was confronted in war, he had to keep his eyes on God even after he prayed to God. Violent acts of destruction and killing one another is not the solution. God has a way of taking care of all enemies. Pray like King Jehoshaphat prayed to God. When anyone goes against God, they will have to answer. Listen, keep your eyes on God and He will take care of your battles and every war anywhere and anytime! God will get the victory.

SHAKE THE DEVIL OFF!

ACTS 28:5 But Paul shook the snake off into the fire and suffered no ill effects.

The Apostle Paul was so confident that the poisonous snake bite was not going to kill him. He did not even flinch. Grown-ups cry at the bite of an ant or a small bug. You have to have some real faith in Jesus to shake off a snake. In basic training, we had something called a shakedown. The shakedown by Drill Sergeant Instructors was necessary for a recruit that just arrived to basic training. This civilian has just signed up to be transformed into a soldier. He must be thoroughly checked for harmful possessions in that environment. In the eight weeks of basic training each soldier has experienced a shakedown at least once each week after training in various areas. I remember that it got easier each time. My discipline and confidence was building each time he told me to drop and move out. I was getting conditioned to shake off anything. This helps me to shake off my old man and start with the new man inside me. In fact, I took on a new mind which is also in Jesus Christ.

The Apostle Paul shook off a snake and the bite. It is unheard of to just shake off a snake and the bite as well. The bite had no effect because he believed in Jesus. God was with Him to shake that venomous bite off. You have received similar bites; we all have, by the enemy who wants to control our lives. One bite by the enemy could destroy you if you allow it. You are going to have to shake off that bad relationship. Shake off diseases, shake off witch craft, shake off that Jezebel spirit, and shake off things that don't line up with the Word. Shake it off in the name of Jesus. Shake it off and suffer no ill effects like the Apostle Paul. Call on Jesus to rescue you. If you don't have Jesus in your life, the enemy is trying to put venom inside your heart to reject Jesus. Call on His name, right now! Ask Him today to be your Lord and Savior. Surrender completely to Him. Today, you need to make a choice because the enemy is not playing with you. He is not joking with you. He is in it for the kill. He wants to steal, kill, and destroy you and your family. Be the priest of your house and stand against it by surrendering yourself first and ask God to cover your family.

STRIPPED AND FAVORED

GEN 37:23-28 So when Joseph came to his brothers, they stripped him of his robe - the richly oriented robe he was wearing. And they took him and threw him into the cistern. Now the cistern was empty; there was no water in it. So when the Midianite merchants came by, his brothers pulled Joseph up out of the cistern and sold him for twenty shekels of silver

to the Ishmaelite, who took him to Egypt.

There is a such thing as stripping a person's dignity from them. In other words, you can break a person if they allow their weakness to take control of their lives. Joseph's brothers tried to break him. It is a crazy thing to know that someone in your own household will try to break you and strip you. Each person knows exactly what their heart is telling them to do. They know! They just keep on doing what the devil tells them because they do not have a relationship with Jesus.

Joseph was stripped by his brothers to be used by God. Joseph's brothers and His entire family did not understand the anointing on his life. They did not have the vision or the dreams he had. Joseph's brothers thought that they had broken his spirit. Instead they just pushed him into the favor of God. They stripped him down for the purpose of getting rid of their father's favorite son. They did not know that by stripping him of the coat of many colors, they set him up for God's favor and blessings at a different level. Don't you worry if someone tried to break you and strip you of your dignity and personal identity. You just stand for Jesus and watch His power work in your life. God has worked it out for you to receive the abundance of favor in your life. Just for your trouble, you will get double. There is no way to stop the blessings that God has in store for you and me. Certainly, Joseph's blessings were not going to be stopped. When the Lord set something in motion, it will not be stopped by anyone or anything. Please understand that the move of God is too powerful for anyone.

Joseph's coat represented royalty. His father gave it to him because he favored him. Joseph coat is viewed as the rainbow for the covenant God made with Noah, no more floods. Some see the coat as a representation of a priest. His father saw it as a gift and a blessing for his son. We need to know that God has made all of us royal priests in His army. We need to know that when we have family situations, God does not turn His back on us. There are blessings on the way. The robe was a blessing and that is exactly why the enemy wanted to twist things in the family, causing jealousy. It is clear that when Jesus rose from the dead He wore a priestly robe.

Jealousy can cause all kinds of trouble. But when trouble comes our way, He always makes everything alright. He walks with us and protects us. The Pharisees were jealous of Jesus because He went about healing, making miracles happen, and teaching disciples. Jesus was punished because of jealousy by the Pharisees and His own people. Joseph was punished by his own brothers. No matter how much you feel like somebody has broken you like a slave, keep your head up and look to the hills from whence comes your help. Jesus always looked up to the Father when things got rough. He prayed in the Garden of Gethsemane. Joseph just kept the faith in knowing who his God was during that time.

DAY 34

GOD KNOWS YOUR WORKS

REV 3:15-16 I know your works, that you are neither cold nor hot, I could wish you were cold or hot. So then, because you are lukewarm, and neither cold nor hot, I will vomit you out of my mouth.

Our Father in heaven knows everything about our works. There is nothing hidden from our heavenly Father. He knows everything. He knows everybody in the five-fold ministry (Ephesians 4:11). He has already assigned you to a good work before the foundations of the world. God knows your ability and talents. Use them for His glory! What are you waiting on? I am inviting you again each Sunday until you commit to Jesus. Let Him into your heart today! You get an invitation every Sunday. Do it now! Sing praises to His name. Our Father in heaven knows everything that goes on in the church and outside the church. Nothing is hidden.

I love sports, but not more than I love my Lord, Jesus Christ. I will skip every game of any kind to get to him and serve Him. In sports, it's kind of crazy because when I was playing, it was easy to be cold and hot. I was hot when I was hitting three pointers against the other team, my enemy! However it gets crazy once the coach takes you out, because he wants to preserve you. But your body gets cold. So, I had to wrap up in my sweats. There were times when I could not get hot like I was. I was lukewarm in which I could not score. At that point, the coach would take me back out. The problem, this time, was I was under performing and waited for a chewing out. The coach knows how to chew you out and spit you up to the point to get your game up. God wants us on fire for Him in the ministry, telling people about the cross, salvation, the resurrection and his miracles as He ministered.

He knows the ability of those who proclaim His name. He knows who has backslidden and fallen from the faith. He knows what caused it and who caused it and the situation behind it. God is no respecter of persons. No one can hide. No one can get away with anything. He is omnipresent. There is nowhere to hide. He is everywhere and all knowing. He is looking for a church without spot or wrinkle. God knows the heart of man. God knows the heart of the Church.

The Lord wants men to have a heart that is on fire for Him. He said, be either cold or hot. The point is to go all the way for Him. He wants men to have a servant's hearts that will continue in obedience. He wants men to follow in His will for their lives and the ministry of the Gospel. You do not have to stand by and let the enemy snatch you away. Listen to the voice of the Lord.

Noah did, he was on fire for the Lord. He built an Ark and saved the world from total devastation. Abraham was on fire. He moved when God told Him to move. He moved in faith and became the Father of many nations. God has something in store for you. You are a child of the Most High, so start walking in the anointing placed in your life.

WORSHIP GOD AND SERVE HIM

Matthew 4:1-12 Then Jesus was led up by the Spirit into the wilderness to be tempted by the devil. And when He had fasted forty days and forty nights, afterward He was hungry. Now when the tempter came to Him, he said, "If You are the Son of God, command that these stones become bread." But He answered and said, "It is written, 'Man shall not live by bread alone, but by every word that proceeds from the mouth of God.' "Then the devil took Him up into the holy city, set Him on the pinnacle of the temple, and said to Him, "If You are the Son of God, throw Yourself down. For it is written:

> **He shall give His angels charge over you, and,**
> **In their hands they shall bear you up,**
> **Lest you dash your foot against a stone.**

Jesus said to him, "It is written again, 'You shall not tempt the LORD your God.'"

> **Again, the devil took Him up on an exceedingly high mountain, and showed Him all the kingdoms of the world and their glory. And he said to Him, "All these things I will give You if You will fall down and worship me." Then Jesus said to him, "Away with you, Satan! For it is written, 'You shall worship the LORD your God, and Him only you shall serve.'Then the devil left Him, and behold, angels came and ministered to Him. Now when Jesus heard that John had been put in prison, He departed to Galilee.**

The enemy wants to steal your worship and service for our Lord, Jesus. Jesus began His Galilean ministry after He fasted for forty days. When you fast and pray, you may have a wilderness experience that will change the course of your life. Jesus had an experience that was set by the Father in heaven. There are advantages as listed below in fasting. One of that stands out is the relationship with Jesus and sincere worship of God.

It appears that one of the most effective ways to begin your ministry is by fasting and praying. This allows you to seek the Lord and get closer to Him. Fasting opens up channels of communication between you and God. You can get properly connected when you leave flesh out. God loves it when we put our agenda aside. He wants us to fast properly by not publicly announcing it. It is personal between you and God alone. God wants us to have breakthroughs. Jesus illustrated exactly what we need to do. We fast and use the word of God against the enemy who chases us daily. We fast to get the mission done. We fast out of devotion to Christ Jesus to let go of things that entangle and bind us. We fast and pray because we are committed to live a life in Christ Jesus.

Today, if you are asking yourself why do I need to fast? You fast to break strongholds, to use your God-given authority, to get closer to God, and have an effective prayer life. Fasting helps you in warfare. If there is something that you can't do without every day (except for water), then it may have a grip on your life. When you fast, get ready for some attacks because you operate in the spirit even more. Also remember that God is on your side whenever you are going through. It is important that you seek God before fasting.

FRUIT OF THE SPIRIT-CHARACTER

GALATIONS 5:21-26 But the fruit of the Spirit is love, joy, peace, longsuffering, kindness, goodness, faithfulness, gentleness, self-control. Against such there is no law. And those who are Christ's have crucified the flesh with its passions and desires. If we live in the Spirit, let us also walk in the Spirit. Let us not become conceited, provoking one another, envying one another.

Everyone must go this route when it comes to patience. You have to have patience in just about all the things you do, especially in raising a family and taking care of the home. You have to be patient with friends, co-workers, church members and basically all people. We tend to want the best seat in the house. Sometimes we have to settle for any seat. We are to be content with what we have in life. Having patience helps us to be content. Patience is needed to be successful. It is definitely a powerful component of the fruit of the Spirit. Patience is the key to many issues in the natural as well as in the spirit or supernatural. Patience is demonstrated when we wait without anger and anxiety. In marriage, we need to let the Holy Spirit work for us when it comes to patience.

More importantly, you have to have patience to walk faithfully in Christ Jesus. The Apostle Paul illustrated in the book of Acts a great deal of patience as he went on several missionary journeys. It was patience that helped him make it through those journeys. Patience helps you to be confident in God in all things, because you will learn to lean on God's strength. It is of the Holy Spirit. Patience helps you understand that you do not have to give in to anything in this world. What will take you over in this life and the life to come is the possession of the Fruit of the Spirit.

DAY 35

NEWNESS OF LIFE

ROMANS 6:4 Therefore we were buried with Him through baptism into death, that just as Christ was raised from the dead by the glory of the Father, even so we should also walk in the newness of life.

In baptism, when we see a person immersed into the water who has received Jesus as Lord and Savior. The person must be aware that the Holy Spirit is present at the rebirth or born again process. This person makes a new commitment to the Lord, Jesus Christ. In baptism, we see a picture of this person being resurrected from the dead. In other words, the old person is left in the watery grave and the new person rises to walk in newness of life in Jesus Christ. This same born again person has demonstrated his obedience by being water baptized which acknowledges that he believes in the death, burial, and resurrection of Jesus Christ our Lord and Savior. He therefore vows to walk in the newness of life because he has a new spirit man, a new relationship, he believes and most of all has completely accepts Jesus Christ as Lord and Savior.

You should obey His command to be baptized in the name of the Father, son and Holy Ghost (Matthew 28). You must stop wavering and doubting in your own selfish and ignorant mentality. This is the proper water baptism period! Why? It is because Jesus said it the method to use. It makes so much since why Jesus wants us to get baptized. The trinity is present in baptism. The trinity is present in Jesus baptism (Matthew 3:13-17).

The newness in life is a brand new life and it starts over because you are associated with Jesus who we know as the King of Kings and Lord of Lord, the Alpha and Omega, the beginning and the end. We are to reign with Jesus. You can be a new person who walks with a new attitude, new joy, a new mind, a new heart, new healing, a new personality, and a new character. You can show love in new ways because you belong to Jesus Christ, the Son of the living God. The old man is passed away and the new man is here to stay now and eternally.

I realize now that I am dead to sin and now quicken in the Spirit of Christ. I am no longer who I used to be. I am a new creature in Christ Jesus. The grave yard not only symbolizes that time is up, it also symbolizes a new life must start. The past life is gone, and more importantly I reign in God's kingdom. I am a new creature in Christ Jesus. I am blessed in Jesus Christ. When Jesus returns, although no man no the time nor the hour, I will be pulled up in the air (raptured) with Jesus (1 Thessalonians 4:13-18).

A FATHER THAT BLESSES YOU!

LUKE 15:15-23 Then he went and joined himself to a citizen of that country, and he sent him into his fields to feed swine. And he would gladly have filled his stomach with the pods that the swine ate, and no one gave him anything. "But when he came to himself, he said, 'How many of my father's hired servants have bread enough and to spare, and I perish with hunger! I will arise and go to my father, and will say to him, "Father, I have sinned against heaven and before you, and I am no longer worthy to be called your son. Make me like one of your hired servants."' "And he arose and came to his father. But when he was still a great way off, his father saw him and had compassion, and ran and fell on his neck and kissed him. And the son said to him, 'Father, I have sinned against heaven and in your sight, and am no longer worthy to be called your son.' "But the father said to his servants, 'Bring] out the best robe and put it on him, and put a ring on his hand and sandals on his feet. And bring the fatted calf here and kill it, and let us eat and be merry

It is absolutely a blessing that we have a Father who blesses us even when we drift off into a world of our own. Always call on the Father in heaven during the time of uncertainty and family difficulty. Never hesitate to think that God is going to rescue you. Only one God will rescue you from any situation and His name is

Jesus Christ. Did you hear that? One God is your rescuer. He is also the best father anyone could have. Make sure you turn to God for everything.

I was thinking of the prodigal son's father who blessed his son upon returning home. The father in this story needed the help of God to be patient and loving in order to bless his son. The father did not look back at his son's past mistakes. He just welcomed him home with open arms. I find that Jesus wants all men to have the spirit of loving their sons and opening their arms wide open to welcome them home. Men do not have to put up with the attacks and manipulation of the enemy, trying to force fathers against sons and sons against fathers. The same applies with mothers and daughters. Ask God, the Father to let His love overpower all the tricks and deception of the enemy. The enemy always tries to get involved when there is love involved. He rises up when there is inheritance involved, you might as well expect to fight the good fight. Whenever seed is involved, you can expect persecution and attacks. Thanks be to God who strengthens us in those weak moments. God will always deliver His people.

BELIEVE

John 20:27-29 Then He said to Thomas, Reach your finger here, and look at My hands; And reach your hand here, and put it into my side. Do not be unbelieving, but believing, And Thomas answered and said to Him, My Lord and My God! Jesus said Thomas because you have seen Me, you have believed. Blessed are those who have not seen and yet believed.

Jesus impacted many people. What was so important about His touch? He always made it personal. Healing was a result of His touch. It was His love that restored every possible issue in His touch. His touch in our lives is the key focus. He touched the blind, the lame, Lepers, broken men, and the dead. He also allowed Himself to be touched. He never denies His unfailing love, grace, mercy and healing power for all people. God desires to touch each one of our lives every day.

You might have a personal experience one day that binds you. But God is able to deliver you from it, because you are His child. He knows if you trust in Him.

It was hard for Thomas for a little while but he came around to understand who Jesus really was at that time. When Thomas saw that Jesus had risen from the dead his faith grew instantly. He believed in the resurrection.

There were men in scripture that had leprosy. These men wanted healing and received it because of Jesus. They believed in Him who cured them. The power of Jesus's love in healing people can change the entire course of your life. These men did not have to be cast out of society any longer. When you ask the Lord to heal you in one area, just get ready because you will be healed in every area. Just ask. The power behind us believing in Him changes everything right now.

DAY 36

ABIDE IN JESUS

JOHN 15:7 "If you abide in Me, and My words abide in you, you will ask what you desire, and it shall be done for you.

I love to use the example of a woman that falls in love with a man or vice-versa the man falls in love with a woman. The two must connect. The intent is to remain together in love with each other. If either of them neglects the other, then your relationship could easily be over. If you desire to make it work, you must show that person love and respect every day. You must become one in their life with them. Blessings flow because you are connected to that person.

Jesus teaches us about abiding in Him. Abiding in Jesus means to remain in Him. As believer, this means that you do not jump in and out of a relationship with Jesus. You need to commit to Jesus. He wants us to be connected to Him as the power source of our lives. If you desire power, then abide in Him. He reveals to us His promise to bless those who abide in Him. He will answer our petitions and fulfill our desires of those who abide in Him. You will be fruitful because you abide in Him. **"If you abide in Me, and My words abide in you, you will ask what you desire, and it shall be done for you."**

Jesus wants us to know that if we trust Him totally with His word, He will bless us more than we can imagine. Abiding in Jesus causes doors to open that were closed. It will produce breakthroughs. You will experience new things in your life. When you abide in Jesus, hell can't hold you. No weapon formed against you will prosper. It will not work against God's chosen ones. His blessings reign in our lives. We need to understand that our God owns everything in this world and the worlds to come. Psalms 37:4 said, "Delight thyself in the Lord, and he shall give thee the desires of thine heart." He is the Creator and can make anything possible that seems impossible. He is the God of the invisible who makes things come to be. So when you are looking at the impossibilities, God is up to something in your life to turn it around. Our Father in Heaven is capable of supplying all of our needs. According to Philippians 4:19, "And My God shall supply all your needs according to His riches and glory by Christ Jesus." We have the word that gives us the answer to all life's problems.

MARRIAGE DEFINED

GENESIS 3:23-24 And Adam said: This is now bone of my bones And flesh of My flesh; She shall be called Woman, Because she was taken out of Man. Therefore a man shall leave his father and mother and be joined to his wife, and they shall become one flesh.

The Bible places marriage as one of the highest areas of life when it comes to relationships. God's involvement is imperative. He is the critical link between the husband and the bride (wife). The Lord must be present in the marriage. A marriage made by God is a marriage made in heaven. Your marriage is covered by God. He is your covering. He is your counselor, psychologist and provider. He equips both of you to love, be intimate, and to comfort one another. God wants to continually bless your marriage. Make sure you surrender it totally to Him. You are obligated to God and your spouse to have a relationship with Jesus Christ as your Lord and Savior. This heavenly marriage through Jesus Christ is better than any love story. It goes beyond fairytales. Here is the key above all! God ordained your marriage. Therefore, give your marriage the highest respect and honor because in doing so you honor God. He created it to be a union between one man and one woman. God established this blessed relationship in the Garden of Eden when he brought Eve to Adam. God blessed marriages as you will see in accordance with Gen 3: 23-24 and Mark 10:6-9. Nothing is to come between your marriage. Please watch the complete book and film that I am surrendering for production. Watch the play that I have produced. God made them specifically for one another. Do not drift into the mindset of what he explains in Romans 1:18-32. Remember above all, the marriage has to be God centered, if you want it to work. Honor must be at the center to God and to each other in respective roles of the marriage. The marriage vows are sacred in the eyes of God and witnesses.

When people fail or step out of true matrimony, they open the gates of hell into their lives and marriage. Love sends the devil back to hell every time.

The enemy starts to feed off of the weakness of people. Then they fall for anything the enemy throws at them. The enemy makes it look good and feel good, then distorts the mind and spirit to making one believe that whatever the sin is, it's good. You need to understand that the enemy is the author of lies and confusion. He wants to destroy your blessed marriage. The one the priest and both of you vowed to live by. Keep your marriage in prayer and before God at all times. He will bless it. You do not have to allow your marriage and yourself to become a tragedy and victim of the enemy. Instead walk in the victory daily under His saving grace and power of love. You deserve to be blessed by God. Your loved ones and all of your family deserve to be blessed. Anyone who walks with God knows that evil exists to tear you apart. The enemy wants to take you over and destroy your loving family. Those that marry outside of God's will are opening themselves up for evil to take over completely. May all of God's people come together on one accord and be blessed by God's true marriage principles.

HIS GOODNESS AND GLORY

EXODUS 33:18-20 And he said, please show me your glory. Then He said I will make all My goodness pass before you, and I will proclaim the name of the Lord before you. I will be gracious to whom I will be gracious, I will have compassion on whom I will have compassion. But He said, you cannot see my face; For no man shall see Me, and live. Read vs. 22-23.

The goodness of God will always fill the heart with unspeakable joy and praise. His glory has all power in it. So when God's makes

His goodness to pass before us, something has to happen. Tears rush out uncontrollably with joy. Moses was a man to encounter such a blessed moment! He saw this manifested goodness and glory of God as the Lord made His goodness to pass before Moses. Think about it! God chose this one single man of God to reveal goodness in Himself. He built His man, Moses, up to show Him that He is his God. You have not worked in vain for me. God made a statement that no other God could do. There is nothing to compare the glory of God to. He expressed His love and compassion.

Read what God says, "I will make my goodness to pass before you." Has anyone ever told you that they had a good side that they could use to pass by you? The only one who ever pass before you and show His glory is God. I believe that God is showing us that He passes before us on so many occasions and we miss His presence. He constantly reveals His glory! He passes before us in the midnight hour when no one else is there to see Him but you and His holy angels.

DAY 37

IF YOU KNEW THE GIFT OF GOD

John 4:9-10 Then the woman of Samaria said to Him, "How is it that You, being a Jew, ask a drink from me, a Samaritan woman?" For Jews have no dealing with Samaritans. Jesus answered and said to her, " If you knew the gift of God, and who it is who says to you, Give me a drink , you would have asked Him, and He would have given you living water.

Tradition was that no one could be around or associate with the Samaritan woman. She clearly understood the distinction and what should take place. What I really like about this passage is that Jesus wanted her to know who He was. However, He also wanted her to know that He accepts her regardless of how many relationships with men she had in the past. He wants her to know that the relationship between her past does not equate to a relationship with Jesus.

Clearly, Jesus wants her to identify who He is so she will have no doubt in her mind that Jesus is from God. She would also be very clear about knowing the gift of God. Jesus is the gift of God and is positioned right in her midst. Jesus wants this Samaritan woman to understand that her life was not over. In fact, her life is starting over again because Jesus is really offering Himself to her. He is also referring to the fact that He alone can give her the living water which is really the Holy Spirit of life, His power and Himself. If you knew the gift of God, life would be changed in your daily walk, worship and your prayer life would be changed to the glory of our Father in Heaven. Jesus is expressing that He can provide anything for her necessity and clean her life up so she does not have to give in to wild lifestyles of multiple men. It comes to a point in life when you have to make a stand for yourself and someone else. Do you know the gift of God? Jesus is the gift of God. The Holy Spirit is the gift of God. His word and power is the gift of God. Stop living beneath your means. Jesus is offering Himself to you as a gift that will change your life forever. Jesus wants you to have self-worth and know that you are valuable to Him. Accept Him as the gift in your life. Allow the Holy Spirit to guide your life.

BLESS SOMEBODY TODAY

LUKE 16: 19-26 "There was a certain rich man who was clothed in purple and fine linen and fared sumptuously every day. But there was a certain beggar named Lazarus, full of sores, who was laid at his gate, desiring to be fed with the crumbs which fell from the rich man's table. Moreover the dogs came and licked his sores. So it was that the beggar died, and was carried by the angels to Abraham's bosom. The rich man also died and was buried. And being in torments in Hades, he lifted up his eyes and saw Abraham afar off, and Lazarus in his bosom. "Then he cried and said, 'Father Abraham, have mercy on me, and send Lazarus that he may dip the tip of his finger in water and cool my tongue; for I am tormented in this flame. But Abraham said, 'Son, remember that in your lifetime you received your good things, and likewise Lazarus evil things; but now he is comforted and you are tormented. And besides all this, between us and you there is a great gulf fixed, so that those who want to pass from here to you cannot, nor can those from there pass to us."

Bless someone today! Do not wait another day! Do it, now. Right after a heartfelt prayer to the living God, Send that gift to a starving child, or a broken woman. Help a brother on the street with no food to eat, or someone in need of medical care. Visit a person hospitalized with cancer or some other medical issue. Encourage a depressed man, woman or child, a suicidal person, or a rape victim. Pray for a broken couple dealing with marriage issues. God can turn all of this around. He uses people that He selects personally to help others. Don't get discouraged because God has a plan to use you. God is a turn it around God. Whatever you do, be like Jesus, not the rich man in the story.

Our behavior with riches can cause us to either bless someone or miss out on having a heart that reflects God's. There are results from God's viewpoint for those in the kingdom of God. This picture of the rich man and beggar reflects two different hearts and behaviors toward God and people. The rich man's behavior is completely selfish and has no measure of godliness in his heart. He simply did not care about anyone, but himself. The beggar named Lazarus had serious physical conditions lying at this gate. He was crippled, unable to move. He appears to be handicapped by his condition and unable to take care of himself. He was reaching out to someone who could help. The rich man would not give in to helping Lazarus. This rich man is a picture of a person who ends up in hades. This word hades has several meanings. One definition calls it the underworld; the abode of the spirits of the dead. It's a Greek term used to denote the deity of the underworld and the dead. According to Dobson et. al (1994) " the Greek meaning is a (state) place of departed souls, hell (Dobson et al., 1994)." "The Hebrew parallel is Sheol (se'ol) (Dobson et al., 1994)."

DAY 38

WHEN I SEE THE BLOOD

EXODUS 12:12-15 "For I will pass through the land of Egypt on that night, and will strike all the firstborn in the land of Egypt, both man and beast; and against all the gods of Egypt I will execute judgment: I am the LORD. Now the blood shall be a sign for you on the houses where you are. And when I see the blood, I will pass over you; and the plague shall not be on you to destroy you when I strike the land of Egypt.

When God speaks He speaks clear, loud, precise, but more importantly He speaks His commands strictly in Holiness, in Spirit and in Truth. He is God and whatever He says will come to pass. He has no respect of persons. His voice will not be mistaken. When God sent Moses to set His people free, He set in motion a plan to free his people from bondage. Nevertheless, the Lord God would change the course of Pharaoh's empire. God's secret weapon was the blood. The blood has life in it. No one and nothing can stop the power in the blood.

Pharaoh was the full representation of evil on the earth during that time period that Israel was in bondage. Thousands were under the influence of Pharaoh's empire.

He used his best taskmasters to drive the people in building the temple. They had to step on straw and dirt to make mortar. He used his taskmasters to drive them with whips and barely gave them any water. When you have lived in captivity, and robbed of your rights, and left with no dignity, it may be then you understand that you need the one and only true God's intervention. Yes, He is able to do abundantly and above and beyond all that we can imagine.

THE VOICE OF GOD

John 10:1-5 My Sheep hear my voice and follow me.

God knows that His sheep can hear His voice. His voice is very clear and unmistakable. Are you ready to hear from God? You need to have God on your side, so you can distinguish God's voice from the enemy's voice. In John 10, Jesus speaks these words "Very truly I tell you Pharisees, anyone who does not enter the sheep pen by the gate, but climbs in by some other way, is a thief and a robber. The one who enters by the gate is the shepherd of the sheep. The gatekeeper opens the gate for him, and the sheep listen to his voice. He calls his own sheep by name and leads them out". You need the Shepherd in your life. When He (The good Shepherd) has brought out all his own, he goes on ahead of them. His sheep follow him because they know his voice. But they will never follow a stranger; in fact, they will run away from him because they do not recognize that stranger's voice. (John 10:1-5).

You need to rebuke the enemy's voice loud and clear. You need to make sure no static waves are interfering when God speaks blessings in your life. God's voice is higher and it is not on man's frequency waves. His voice has divine frequency power and blessings. His voice never fails. By the way, when God speaks to His sheep they know His voice and they follow Him. There are distinct blessings and power in His voice that over shadows the enemy's voice. There is power in His word. God does a great deal of speaking in the Bible. In fact, God spoke to Moses on Mount Sinai and other places. God spoke to Isaiah regarding healing Hezekiah to add fifteen more years to his life. God spoke to Ezekiel about raising dead bones that represent Israel in a valley to bring the church back to life. When something is dead, God's voice can bring it back to life. Jesus spoke and called Lazarus back to life. When you are in Jesus Christ even death can't hold you down. His voice has complete power that works.

DAY 39

JESUS HELPS ME STAND!

Jude 1:24-25 Now to Him who is able to keep you from stumbling, And to present you faultless Before the presence of His glory with exceeding joy, To God our Savior, Who alone is wise, Be glory and majesty, Dominion and power, Both now and forever. Amen.

The author Jude, who is the brother of James and the half-brother of Jesus, writes in this book about the infiltration of false teachers. He also points out that these false teachers are causing division and promoting much inappropriate theology. They also demonstrate destructive and prideful behavior. These are elements that can corrupt a church and persuade babes in Christ to fall away and potential clients to walk away and miss out of salvation.

The good news is that God is able to keep us from falling. The word falling means in this passage, stumbling. God always keeps us from stumbling into the enemy's hands. Jude is talking about spiritually stumbling. It always takes Jesus to help us regain our balance. Instead of being spiritually clumsy and falling into the hands of the enemy, He wants to catch us and save us; to present us faultless before the presence of His glory. Don't worry about being embarrassed. Jesus is our Savior and he is the only wise God that has dominion and power. Have you ever stumbled and hit rock bottom due to life difficulties? Jesus is our Savior and His arms are wide open to save you right now. Your life will never be the same. If you believe you fell out of relationship with Jesus Christ, You have a chance today, Ask Him for forgiveness and to come into your heart. Jesus is there to run off any principalities and rulers of dark places that has intentions to take you from Jesus.

Today, you need to call on the name of Jesus in prayer. He saves no matter what! He has the power to help you stand and live a blessed life.

BLESSED IN EVERY AREA

DEUTERONOMY 28 And it shall come to pass, if thou shalt hearken diligently unto the voice of the Lord thy God, to observe and to do all his commandments which I command thee this day, that the Lord thy God will set thee on high above all nations of the earth: And all these blessings shall come on thee, and overtake thee, if thou shalt hearken unto the voice of the Lord thy God. Blessed shalt thou be in the city, and blessed shalt thou be in the field.

As God's people we need to obey the voice of God and receive His blessings. Then we need to do what he states in His commands. One of the most powerful stories in the Bible is the story of Noah and the ark he built for God. It was built because he hearkened to the voice of the Lord.

We are blessed emotionally, physically, spiritually, financially, in the body of Christ. God overtakes the believer who trusts in Him and will receive His best blessings. They are accessible to you. God is telling you that you can't miss His blessings. The abundance of blessings are flowing when we demonstrate to God the obedience of our hearts. God reveals to us in Deuteronomy 28 the blessings available to those who will hearken diligently to His word, He also reminds us that curses are here, as well, if we do not obey his commands. No one else has the power to bless you, but God. The next time you get ready to get out of alignment with God, because a friend ask you to do something unethical, shake it off. Let that friend know that your life has changed and that you walk in the blessed life in Jesus Christ.

DAY 40

VICTORY IS IN JESUS CHRIST!

1 JOHN 5:4-5 For whatever is born of God overcomes the world. And this is the victory that has overcome the world-our faith. Who is he who overcomes the world, but he who believes that Jesus is the son of God.

Faith is powerful. Believing that Jesus is the Son of God is the most powerful thing you can do. It's your entry way into salvation and Heaven. Believing that Jesus is the Son of God gets the Father's attention. The problem in society is that you can just about believe in anything. Most people believe in things that have a hold on them. They believe in other spiritual things: like voodoo, witchcraft, cults, scientology, and other evil things. Don't play around with those deadly idols and spirits. Don't even give into traditional things as well that will grip your heart and spirit man. Get Jesus Christ, the Son of God in your life today. Surrender to Jesus now! Find a Bible and read Romans 10:9-10 today. You have access on your cell phone, computer and your Bible. Please hurry and read it. Then kneel in prayer and say to Jesus, "I repent of my sin, I believe you died on the cross and rose from the dead. Please come into my heart right now. I accept you as my Lord and Savior. I receive you right now in Jesus name, Amen." When you believe and accept Jesus Christ in your heart, you have the victory.

To be born of God already reflects that you have the victory in the Lord. No one can walk victorious without Him. You must be born again to walk in victory. You must have faith to be an overcomer of the world. The world is tricky because it is attractive and lures people into evil. The world is filled with enticing things that look so good. You need to make Jesus look good and make Him the head of your life today. Without Jesus in your life, it's like committing spiritual suicide. He will bring you out of any condition and bless you. Stop allowing people to predict what your spiritual relationship is supposed to be. The fact is you were created for God's purpose. Start talking to God daily. If you feel like you are a back slider, a person never fully committed to Jesus, then recommit your life now. Go to church and do it publicly and/or open Romans 10:9 repent of your sin and read the scripture and tell Jesus you agree and believe that he died on the cross and rose from the dead. Ask Him to come into your heart. Then you can tell any and everybody that no one can snatch victory away from you because of who you are now.

Victory comes directly from Jesus. He has defeated death, the grave and the devil. Our strength, knowledge, skills, and our creativity all come from God.

AGREE!

Matthew 18:19 Again I say unto you, That if two of you shall agree on earth as touching anything that they shall ask, it shall be done for them of my Father which is in heaven.

The Lord is pleased when He observes His saints in agreement. One of the strongest examples of being in agreement was on the day of Pentecost. The scripture in Act 2:1-6 says, When the day of Pentecost arrived, they were all together in one place. And suddenly there came from heaven a sound like a mighty rushing wind, and it filled the entire house where they were sitting. And divided tongues as of fire appeared to them and rested on each one of them. And they were all filled with the Holy Spirit and began to speak in other tongues as the Spirit gave them utterance. Now there were dwelling in Jerusalem Jews, devout men from every nation under heaven. And at this sound, the multitude came together, and they were bewildered, because each one was hearing them speak in his own language (Acts 2:1-6).

It is important to be in agreement because God shows up and something happens. These people spoke in tongues as evidence of being filled in the spirit. God's presence was upon them and their lives were changed. Agreement is just that important. In another respect, agreement must be in the home with husband and wife. The wife needs to consult her God and husband so they can be on one accord. If a wife ventures off into agreement with another party, and put them above her husband, she then allows another spirit (such as a jezebel, witchcraft or demonic spirit) to manipulate her marriage. Her husband is the head and she can't change that! She should accept the blessing of him being her covering and protector. The same applies to the husband with his dependency of her filling the role of wife. Agreement is personal and must be taken seriously. Agreement is for the purpose of hearing from our God in heaven. We, on the receiving end, await God's approval on whatever the request is. We must be lined up and on one accord in reverence to God. Whatever you agree on make sure it is only to the glory of God! In Jesus name Amen.

ACCOUNTABLE

Luke 12:48 But someone who does not know, and then does something wrong, will be punished only lightly. When someone has been given much, much will be required in return; and when someone has been entrusted with much, even more will be required.

If you have ever seen a professional athlete in action operating at their peak, it's because of accountability. A professional player is expected to perform at their best. That, my friend, is accountability (player to coach, and coach to owner). Accountability is important in the sports world.

If you are living in this world today and have a family, you are accountable to your family. God holds us accountable. The man is the spiritual head and covering of his wife and children. He must make sure the children are being respectful and obeying their parents. The wife is accountable as being a helpmeet. This marriage must line up with 1 Corinthians 7, Matthew 12, Mark 10, and Ephesians 5. The children must line up with Ephesians 6. When they read about living a long life dependent on your obedience to God, they will be amazed at God's words. Accountability is a good thing because it allows us to remove pride. It also enables us to have someone to check on us and keep us on spiritual track. We need to be foremost accountable to reading and studying God's word. The word of God is life (Hebrews 4:11-16) Jesus holds all of His disciples accountable (Ephesians 4:11-12) (Hebrews 6, 7).

THE GENUINE GOD RUNNER

Fiction Story

INTRODUCTION

The City of New York is in a panic for the next huge explosion which has led them to believe that the world was ending. Jack Steele knows immediate action is needed to help this city survive attacks. It's a sacrifice and challenge to save the city of Manhattan, New York and get it restored. Terror Man is a villain (evil spirit) that can transform into darkness. This spirit man is an executioner of innocent people and has taken over the city and has everyone fleeing into hiding and abandoning everything to save their lives. Terror Man is holding people hostage and executing people as well. Jack sees him on several fronts attacking.

Jack must confront Terror Man and his demons by fighting to the end in the city and on the battlefield. There is no compromise. Jack realizes that Terror Man has no remorse for anyone. He sets out to kill entire families in the city, like the devil he truly is. His plots and motives are to destroy the world. He has found ways to access nuclear weapons and secret atomic bombs to take out this city, the White House, and multiple neighboring states. Jack will do all he can to keep evil from harming and taking over the city. He will need help. His greatest weapon is God on His side. The enemy doesn't take into account that Jack is a man appointed by God to take this mission and win as many souls as possible as he fights to help restore the city from all manners of evil. Watch how many people come to God for salvation after Jack's witness and strength in the Lord to help others. Jack will be known as the God Runner.

BACKGROUND

Terror man is stalking his home and wife. Jack would soon find out that a large amount of money is hidden. It is from the 40 year old robbery that took place in the old Belmont National Bank. Nevertheless, The Blazer and his crew failed to anticipate the presence of a holy angel sent by God on Jack's side. Jack was only an infant when these villains broke into the home and murdered his parents as the city had erupted in unlimited crime and chaos. Leaders in the city had been over run, violated, held hostage, and placed in a prison cell for the next few years. Jack has grown up now. He has business to handle.

This character, TERROR MAN has created a design and plan to take over the city as he temporarily holds Jack hostage in a pit surrounded by other demons. Jack is never alone. The Terror Man is an evil person with demonic powers and appearance. The Terror Man's background: He came to be because he was terrorized in his life by greedy gangsters and those that claimed to be good leaders. He lived in torment for years as he grew up with more hate. They were crooked and terrorized his family and tortured him. This caused his heart to turn evil. He could only think terror. So after a few fights, he swore to pay back in the worst way by causing devastating disaster in the city and taking over the world with a special atomic bomb and secret chemicals hidden in the lab. The Terrorizer came from a life of crime and believes that everyone owed him something. Because he felt that life was not fair to him, he became a harden criminal. He was beaten by gangs and left to die, as fire took hold of the building he was beaten and robbed in. The fire consumed him and a spirit came over and he made pact to serve that spirit if it protected him from death. It was a dark spirit that made him commit to crime; he was indebted to Terror Man.

START

COL Jack Steele, the God Runner, finds himself in a situation where he sees devastation happening all around. He can't hold back in helping society. He first sees it in the city. However, he had previously enlisted into the military as an officer. He has no option but to take a stand against crime and violence in the city as well as what happens on the battlefield. It has impacted innocent families. The Terrorizer is taking innocent families and enslaving them as he places them into camps and prisons for his pleasure. The Terrorizer and his men are involved in all kinds of terrorism and crime, government deals, security breaches, and world dominance. What is worse is they want to get their hands on the code for an atomic bomb to destroy nations and bring about world wars and destruction. Jack has to fight to protect secret codes in the hands of government officials. He is up against all of Terrorizers men, evil spirits and corrupted officials. Jack fights on behalf of the country to bring down this evil. Jack is a Soldier with special skills to fight this enemy. Most of them are so corrupted and evil that they have no regard for innocent people and the poor. He opens up with Jack in his earlier years of life noticing the destruction all around. Jack takes care of business duty wise on the battlefield as a Black Hawk pilot. Then he comes back home to fight battles with God on his side.

COMBAT OPERATIONS
BLACK HAWK

COL. Jack Steele is flying a Black Hawk in combat, where the mission is in a hot zone in Baghdad. The terrain is open as the aircraft zeroes in on its targets and opens fire. It takes out two high intelligence points and one key leader cell. This is a high risk rescue operation. Terrorist and evil enemy eyes take note of the actions of COL Jack Steel because he has made a name for himself. Jack is a Godly man and at the same time a soldier on the battlefield.

SPECIAL SPIRITUAL SKILL

COL. Jack Steele is endowed with special skills. This is his last week in combat operations. He has also just got selected for an emergency mission. Jack accepts to go on this mission because it's all about rescue, savings lives. The Terrain is tough and hard to navigate. In addition to this there are crucial and complicated areas to infiltrate. COL Jack Steele signals to his Black Hawk crew to take over his skill set. He is also highly spiritual and relies on God in his life for strength. He is a real strategic thinker and planner. On the command using a secret password, his team, MAJ Baines and Chief (CW5) Dixon came to conduct a proper rescue approach and formation at the pickup points of rescue. Faced with heavy weapon fire and much combat smoke, COL. Jack Steele aircraft goes low again. He spots CPT Baxter and his team. He then dives low to pick up point as comrades on board maintain suppressive fire destroying enemy targets using the aircraft rockets launcher and weapons systems. "CPT Baxter, let's go, now!" said COL. Jack Steele. CPT Baxter is the last one pulled in after his scout team is loaded with two aircraft. The rescue is a success. The Black Hawk moves to get out of area with speed and fire power and agility. CPT Baxter tells Jack that another scout team is out there in their vicinity. As his aircraft pulls away, he notices an image that is moving along the battlefield killing everything in its path. He can't put his finger on it. It's dark and evil. This enemy is the Terror Man who is a dark spirit. In other appearances he wears a mask covering his head completely. On the battlefield he unleashes his evil spirits (demons).

Jack Steele saw things that no one else could see in the spirit. He is gifted to see those things in the spirit as God allows Him to see. The Terror Man was wreaking havoc along the battlefield and back at home. Once Jack Steele gets CPT Baxter's team to the Black Hawk, he returns down below where other soldiers were taking on heavy fire. He saw what appeared to be a demonic spirit chasing and killing men. As a demon confronts him and almost snatches Jack's life, God's angel rescues him and defeats the demonic spirits right on the spot. From that time on Jack has gotten closer to God. He feels a since of connection to warn other people and tell of the saving grace of God. Jack completes his mission and retires from the Armed Forces.

RETIREMENT CEREMONY

The retirement ceremony is held at Fort Hood, Texas military base, parade field. Jack spent most of his military career here and his family was living here. He is headed back to New York upon completion of the ceremony. The retirement ceremony was huge with over 75 Soldiers retiring with the Commanding General and the Command Sergeant Major as the head of the ceremony. Jack receives his award and his ex-wife and children, Walter and Maria, are present to congratulate their dad for all of those years, 28 to be exact. COL Jack Steele receives the Medal of Honor at this ceremony as well as his regular retirement. His wife is there as he requested. Sarah Steele kisses Jack upon his receipt of his retirement certificate presented by the Commanding General. Jack is responsible for destroying key enemy strongholds and rescuing more than 7,000 Soldiers in various circumstances in the military. Jack returns home where he is needed.

JACK AT HOME FROM WAR

Back stateside, Jack met a few buddies at a bar later after the ceremony. After drinking, which is out of the norm for Jack and definitely a setup, Jack awakes and finds himself tied up in a room and being tortured by Terror Man (Mask). Jack is sitting in a chair in the center of the room, handcuffed with his hands behind his back, beaten half dead. God wants him to know that it's not over yet. He has a special assignment. Gabriel is his assigned angel. Gabriel flies off from heaven after appearing before God. Jack can't believe what he is seeing. Gabriel appears before him and heals his wound and re-energizes Jack's spirit man and protects him. Gabriel's mission was to come to earth and be Jack's guardian angel through this cycle of life. Jack is a winner already because he has an angel on his side from God. The Terror Man has underestimated God's plan.

BACK AT JACK'S HOUSE

Jack notices someone with a gun on his balcony. He saw him through the mirror. He plays it off. Jack Steele walks casually in the other room as not to alert the burglar. But the burglar comes out and jumps him immediately, trying to kill him. They are entangled. The burglar has a firm grip around Jack's throat. But Jack manages to break loose and the burglar runs for his life. Jack did not realize with all the adrenaline flowing that he was stabbed in the side and bleeding heavily. Gabriel blocked the knife from stabbing Jack in the heart. The burglar runs out the lower level and breaks a window getting out. Meanwhile Jack reaches for his pistol in the secret compartment. He runs out to catch him; and shoots. The burglar got away too fast. Shots were fired and the police arrived at his home. A report was filed but Jack did not get a good look at the burglar because he had a tight mask on, even though they scuffled.

Jack finds himself in a chase to catch this killer sent by terrorizer Jack and the criminal driver go back and forth to avoid hitting other cars. A few cars flipped over and crashed. They exchanged gun fire from both cars. A helicopter comes in to fire to eliminate Jack. The burglar got away but it's not over. Jack had to avoid a car filled with a mother and three children and a bus filled with passengers. He gets out and looks to see where this car could have vanished so fast. Jack returns home and sends in a call to the chief of polices phone. He then gets some rest and waits for the next day.

JACK AT WORK OFFICE

Jack Steele is at work the next morning. As he walks in, he notices an unfamiliar face. He says to himself that he does not recognize this gentleman. Ms. Alice Richardson, the secretary is sitting at her desk then greets Jack, and then she brings coffee. "Alice, who is the gentleman that just left out of your area?" Alice replied, "What gentleman? No man has been here." "You have to be kidding me. He was just there. I did not see a ghost." The man is waiting outside to make an attempt to get the bag that Jack forgot to give Mr. David Hanson two days ago. He is actually trying to kill Jack and get possession of some top secret material. Jack says, "Who are you looking for, sir?" The strange man answers, "I am from the Daily Journal News. I am a news reporter looking for your CEO to do a story." Jack gives a look like, 'I know you're lying', but plays along. "Well make an appointment at the front desk." Jack is leaving; the man walks behind him and takes out an automatic machine gun as Jack moves to the elevator. Ms. Sharon Davis is screaming and people are ducking and diving to the floor. Some are running out of the building, some being sawed down by this evil man. The man is hit several times after firing at Jack. Three security guards were hit with rounds. After Jack shoots and wounded him, he searches his pockets. He found a mysterious code book and information about him.

This code book mentions atomic bomb. Detective Larry Miller shows up. "Sir", referring to Jack, "I am Detective Miller; I need to have a word with you. Can you tell me what happened?" Jack said, "It was simple, this man was following me and tried to kill me." Detective Miller asked, "Do you know him or have you ever met him before? Jack states, "No I have never seen him and do not know him." Detective Miller asked, "Do you know anyone who holds a grudge and is out to harm your family?" Jack says, "No."

BRIDGE DISCOVERY

Jack receives a call in his office that a murder took place and it's a friend of his. Jack goes to the blue den river about 8 miles from his office. He manages to get there before detectives arrive. He sees a woman's body wrapped up. He hesitates to go over and view the body. Jack knows this lady. This particular incident impacted him in a sad way. He met this young lady before in college! In fact, she was a close friend from many years ago. He really beats himself up about her. Jack goes to the church where he could find emotional and spiritual comfort from God. The police are all over the place trying to find evidence of what happened to this 24 years old student from the local university. Just a few weeks ago, it was another beautiful woman, around 22 years old, a model of the Dynasty Modeling Agency. Detective Miller is on the scene asking questions. Across the street a suspicious character looks on and tries to walk away in his disguise. Jack gets a glance and acts as though he was not going to bother him. Jack drives off and catches Ralph Myers around the corner. He questions him about the murder and asks if he has seen anything. Jack says, "Where do you live and how often do you come this way? Ralph says, "I just happened to come by this way and noticed all the cars. I have nothing to do with this." Jack asked, did you see anything at all suspicious?" Ralph says, "No. I told you, I was not here when this happened. I try my best to stay away from police officers. They are crooked. " Jack said, "I just need your help. I can't be concerned about your feeling of police officers. We have a crisis out here we need to fix." All of a sudden, a shot rings from a building across the street. Ralph goes down to the ground, hit in the chest. Jack takes cover and starts to treat Ralph immediately while his ambulance is on the way. Jack proceeded to the building. The gunman runs and Jack meets this gunman at the top floor. The man falls from the roof as they scuffle. Jack tried to catch him but he could not hold on. The ambulance shows up and the man is transported. Detective Miller is at the hospital to question him if he comes back. The killer is in the hallway at University Hospital waiting to make a move. He is monitoring where the police go so he can track down the person he wants to kill.

KILLERS ON THE LOOSE IN THE HOSPITAL!

Jack Steele makes eye contact with the shooter. Then he chases the shooter out of the hospital to the front entrance. The shooter gets to the entrance faster and evaded the area. Jack goes out the door and around the corner alley to see if there is a trace of him. Jack walks into a set up around the corner where three of men from Terror Man attempts to kidnap Jack. Big Jake tells Jack that" we are going to rip you apart." "You should have stayed out of it" Billy Joe tells Jack. "After we kill you we are going to your house. Oh, we already have that covered. Your wife should be very comfortable by now with the gentlemen we have there. We can avoid all of this if you just tell us where the nuclear code is. We know that you work for the firm". Jack says "I tell you what, if you beat me, you can have the code". The fight starts, Jack uses martial arts and defeats each man very fast. A surprise from the fifth man with a club appeared and could have easily killed Jack. Gabriel steps in and breaks the killing club. Jack still passed out unconscious until he arrived at Terror Man's hideout. Gabriel brings Jack back to consciousness and life! Jack is now transported with a blind fold on to a huge area with darkness (a huge indoor stadium) where all of Terror Man's operations happen.

PEOPLE RESCUED

Once Jack is delivered to the plant, he exits the van with some help. Once the blind fold was off, he looks around and wow! Jack moves through the back entrance chasing Terrorizer. From a distance, he notices an opening that looks suspicious. Jack and Robert discover an entryway that leads to the imprisonment area of people. Terrorizer's plan was to continue torturing people because he can. They cautiously went into the stadium lower hidden offices. Jack says, "Blue, cover my back on this end." "Go, I have you covered," said Blue. Jack keeps going. He halts after receiving a signal that the CPT had men on the way to secure the area. Jack discovers money laundering and deals that were working out. Jack takes the right turn Roger takes the left. Smith takes the center entrance. Jack keeps going and hears some crying sounds. One woman hears footsteps and instinctively shouts, "Help!" To Jack's amazement he discovers families, more than 300 people are down here due to the Terrorizers hit men. Most often they were tied up, felt broken and seemed to have been administered a drug. "Blue, Help me on the count of three to break every chain on each individual so they can be free of tragedy." Jack responds to everyone, "We are here to help you out of this situation. Don't worry. Mike call the police and FBI now! Give our location. However, let's continue to search this area." To their amazement, they located something very crucial.

MANIPULATE SCIENCE

Jack locates different operations as well that Terror man has going on inside the stadium. He has some scientist on his payroll. This science will take him over the top. Jack discovers that Terrorizer is converting peoples mind in an operating room by implanting some kind of specialized chip he has invented. His goal is to discredit God. The Terrorizer thinks that he is a god! Jack comes in just in time to break this mind transformation operation that would put people under his control to do evil acts. They would be led by this chip to commit deadly acts against those in the city. The Terrorizer is one of the enemies working against God and the city of New York. He is working specific details to change the minds of woman.

The Terrorizer is using a process to start a new society and world. After months of kidnapping and taking over the city, he has started the real world integration of the new woman with chips and an alteration of the mind. Jack was too late. Some of the women have already been disposed secretly before he could get there. A Scientist named Dr. Edwin Banks had discovered a chip with special powers to control people and has activated it to the advantage of Terrorizer and his operation. The Terrorizer has forced him to put women back in the society and let them blend in and populate. He has a hidden tracking device for all of them with codes. Dr. Banks tells Terrorizer that "We can make over 2 billion dollars by creating this industry that has never been tapped into", says Dr. Banks. "I agree," says Terrorizer. "We will rule the world and be rich! You just take care of the project and I will take care of Jack Steele and these detectives. When I finish with them they will never bother us again. The Terrorizer plans to attack Jack's family. What he failed to recognize is that Jack had a backup plan with the FBI on his side and they all captured the Terrorizer's worst men. It's not over because he attacks Jack's family.

SARAH'S GRADUATION PARTY

Jack Steele breaks away and shows up at his sister's home. He attended a birthday celebration for his sister. They were out cooking on the deck as the Terrorizer has sent 30 of his best men to take Jack's family out while they were celebrating Sarah's achievement in getting her PHD at Harvard in Forensic Psychology. Sarah is his baby sister. She is 32 years old. Jack had some friends at his sister's house and they discerned the attack and were able to open up fire and fight back against these hit men. Sarah's husband was hit in the arm. One of Jacks friends was hit in the shoulder. All survived after taking out these hit men. Jack made sure his buddies and his brother n law got to the hospital and were treated for minor injuries. The Terrorizer's men lost and some managed to get away. Gabriel stepped right in the front of weapon aimed directly at Jacks head and was fired. Gabriel stopped the bullet. Jack is still living for a purpose. Carlos saw it and could not believe his eyes. Jack explains some of it. "Man, you just received a real miracle Jack," Carlos says, "I know that I am attending church tomorrow. I have to honor God."

NEW JERUSALEM FAITH CENTER CHURCH SERVICE

Jack and a few buddies, Sarah and her family attend church service on Sunday at New Jerusalem Faith Center because God has been too good in their lives. Jack Steele realizes that God gave him an angel to protect his life during these attempts on his life and the people of the city. Jack was successful in rescuing thousands of people. Jack and his wife also recovered the money that was hidden for 40 years and the city rewarded it to those that lost family members.

The Pastor preached his sermon on "A Man full of Faith in God." The Pastor spoke out of the book of Genesis regarding Abraham. God used Abraham to exercise a level of faith and obedience that He really expects from all men. God does not limit His faith. God simply wants us to possess the character that Abraham possessed. Simply put, when God asks you to trust Him, he wants your faith to be pure faith. Know that God hears you. Be the kind of person that will move when God speaks to you. Don't over react to evil but you can react by calling on Jesus, the name above every name. He came from the same God that call Moses out of his comfort zone, the same God who called Jonah to preach repentance to a broken sinful city called Nineveh that he could have easily destroyed. He is the same God who told Abraham to leave his home, knowing all along that Abraham's obedience and faith would help him capture God's heart and help his family overcome struggles, and receive blessings in the land flowing with milk and honey. The choir sings a song, "Nobody told me that road would easy. I've come too far from where I started from." Then they sing another selection, called "Stomp." This song implies to step on the enemy's head. So then put the enemy under your feet (Ephesians 1:22-23).

THE AUTHOR

Joseph Harris currently lives in Texas. He is retired from the United States Armed Forces. However, he continues to work in support of wounded soldiers returning from war.

He is the Pastor and Founder of Christian Worship Outreach Center Ministries. His mission is to preach the Gospel of Jesus Christ! Pastor Harris is Kingdom Focused! His primary focus and foundation is the word of God. He is a Kingdom Builder. He delights in introducing others to receive Jesus Christ, as Lord and Savior.

Pastor Harris is a husband and father. He is also the author of several other books: Transformation Man, Man under Construction, Rock the Pedestal, and Fallen Scales.

Bibliography

Dobson E.G., Feinberg, C.L., Hindson, E.E. Kroll, W. M., & Willmington H.L., (1994).Parallel Bible Commentary. The complete King James Version, p 2438.

www.ingramcontent.com/pod-product-compliance
Lightning Source LLC
Chambersburg PA
CBHW072143160426
43197CB00012B/2227